CHOOSING TO RUN

DES LINDEN

WITH BONNIE D. FORD

CHOOSING
TO RUN

A MEMOIR

DUTTON

DUTTON

An imprint of Penguin Random House LLC
penguinrandomhouse.com

DUTTON and the D colophon are registered trademarks of Penguin Random House LLC.

LIBRARY OF CONGRESS CATALOGING-IN-PUBLICATION DATA

Names: Linden, Des, 1983– author.
Title: Choosing to run : a memoir / Des Linden.
Description: New York, N.Y. : Dutton, [2023] |
Identifiers: LCCN 2022038181 (print) | LCCN 2022038182 (ebook) |
ISBN 9780593186640 (hardcover) | ISBN 9780593474600 (signed edition) |
ISBN 9780593186657 (ebook)
Subjects: LCSH: Linden, Des, 1983– | Marathon running. |
Women long-distance runners—United States—Biography.
Classification: LCC GV1061.15.L57 A3 2023 (print) |
LCC GV1061.15.L57 (ebook) | DDC 796.42092 [B]—dc23/eng/20220917
LC record available at https://lccn.loc.gov/2022038181
LC ebook record available at https://lccn.loc.gov/2022038182

Printed in the United States of America
1st Printing

BOOK DESIGN BY KATY RIEGEL

For everyone brave enough

to lace up and take the first step

and with affection and respect for

Gabe Grunewald (1986–2019)

Gloria Ratti (1931–2021)

CONTENTS

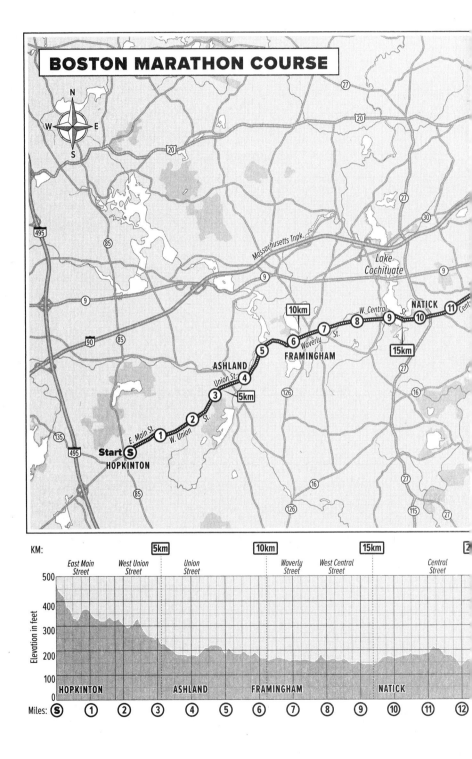

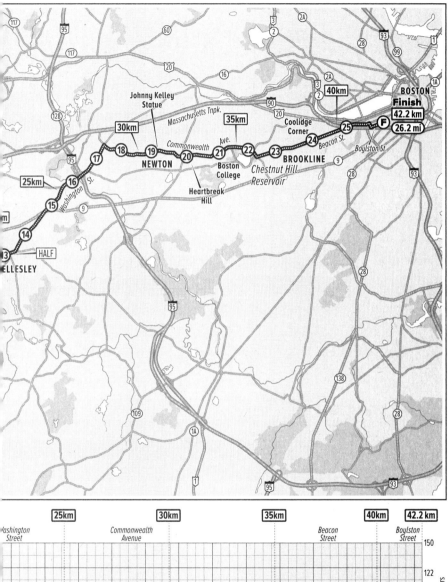
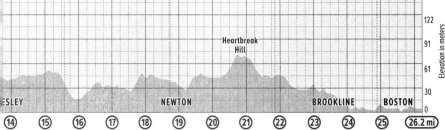

CHOOSING TO RUN

PROLOGUE

I'M ALONE, OUT front.

I've just dropped the only woman between me and the 2018 Boston Marathon finish line. I brace for her to respond, to reappear in my peripheral vision.

I hold my breath—not an advisable tactic at Mile 22—and I count.

One . . . two . . . three . . . four . . . five.

Nothing. Still by myself.

I exhale, releasing months of tension. Young Kenyan runner Gladys Chesir has been aggressive for most of this race. If I can't hear her footfalls on my heels by now, that means she's vulnerable. It's time to ratchet up the pace and inflict pain.

I've visualized this scene, taking the lead coming off Heartbreak Hill, thousands of times over the last decade. I've pictured myself strong, confident, and pulling away under a brilliant blue April sky to win one of the most prestigious marathons in the world.

This moment looks nothing like that.

Rain is sluicing down in sheets, relentless. A fierce headwind batters my face, my chest, my quads. My hands are numb, and my feet are beyond sodden. There's only a scattering of people watching by the side of the road, and if they're cheering, the sound is muted by my drenched headband.

And yet. This is where I've always wanted to be. It's a rare juncture in any career, and there's no guarantee it'll ever happen again. I have to yank myself out of my old sunsplashed dreamscape and be fully present here, now. I need to adapt to the opportunity that has opened up in front of me, on this course I know by heart.

It's been a scant few hours since I stood barefoot in my darkened hotel room, completely devoid of hope, feeling none of the tenacity that had always defined me. I had arrived in Boston without my usual game plan to maximize my chances for a win. My typical meticulous checklist was down to one item: survive.

THAT ALL SHIFTED after the start gun, with absolutely no planning on my part. Improvisation has brought me this far. Now it's time to channel the instincts and knowledge I've sharpened and stowed away over twenty years. I've run thousands of miles so I would know what to do in the next four.

I press the Play button in my head and hear the voice of Frank Browne, my high school coach in California, whose combination of drive and irreverence once pulled the best out of me.

"I know you have the ability. One day you're going to be in position and say, 'Fuck it,' and pull the trigger on one of these races."

I let out another deep, explosive exhale. My mind clears of everything but one thought:

Can I win this thing?

THE OUTSIDER

IT WAS MY fault I was finishing up my last mile in the dark. My dad had pestered me all day about getting the run in, and out of spite, I'd procrastinated. The sun was setting by the time he drove me to the Silver Strand, a scenic sandbar that connects the towns of Imperial Beach and Coronado, just south of San Diego. People were packing up and leaving the beach, wiped out from hours of soaking in the sun and playing in the waves, as I started out on the flat north-south road. He followed me on his bike to keep me company.

I was running at a good clip about five miles into an eight-mile run when I realized I hadn't heard the sound of my dad's wheel for at least ten minutes. I knew one of his tires was losing air, and he'd been working hard to keep up with me. I could have stopped and waited for him to fix it; instead, I decided to press harder, to make him hurt, to make him worry about me being out there by myself. I leaned into the pace a little bit more, visualizing how I'd close out a race at the high school state meet. My dad was the chasing pack, and I was laying on the gas, putting them away for good.

I was so deep in my race dream by the time I hit the parking lot where we'd begun that I almost missed it in the pitch-black. Once I slowed down and walked a few strides to catch my breath, I felt a deep sense of accomplishment about putting in the miles. I was glad I hadn't talked myself out of it. My dad had said that would happen the whole time he was pushing me to get out the door, but I would never tell him he was right. I sat on the curb next to his truck in satisfied silence. Fifteen minutes later, I began to hear the telltale squeak and the faint thud of a flat tire.

◆　◆　◆

BY THEN, I already had a long, complicated competitive history with my dad, Dennis. Growing up, my older sister, Natalie, and I were required to play sports year-round so that we'd be too busy to get in trouble, insulated from a world our parents viewed as full of bad influences and dangerous pitfalls. We didn't have the luxury of taking a season off, for fear that we'd become lazy, and we were expected to be willing to try it all.

Dad scoured the newspaper for new activities, then woke

us up first thing on Saturday morning to tell us what he'd signed us up for: golf lessons one week, coed T-ball the next. From the time I joined my first organized soccer team at age six, he held his own clinics for us after he got off his job as a construction worker—post-practice practices, as we thought of them. We did soccer drills, kicking a size 3 ball against the low retaining wall that bordered our front yard in San Diego while he barked instructions, or juggling the ball with our feet to master the ideal first touch. He coached our softball team, and when Natalie decided she wanted to pitch, I was happy to be her personal catcher. These were not casual sessions; they were about self-improvement, not enjoyment. He'd snap if we weren't being serious enough in his eyes, like the time he ripped into Natalie for smiling too much as she tried to throw strikes. We were close in every way, born just eighteen months apart, and she was perfect in my mind—beautiful, adventurous, better at sports than I was. I couldn't understand why he would criticize her for something that had nothing to do with how well she was pitching. I hunkered down, hiding behind my catcher's mask, thinking, *What level of fun are we allowed to have?* He wouldn't let it go and kept antagonizing her all evening. I had learned not to argue. We kept working hard to appease him and meet his demands to be aggressive on the field, to earn more playing time, to avoid embarrassing him.

Our mom, Nancy, had a more passive, level personality

but was just as committed to our sporting life. She built her entire schedule around us, punching in for her shift as an AT&T operator at five in the morning so that she'd be off in time to pick us up from school, shuttle us to practices and games, and watch and critique every moment of play. In the ultimate parental sacrifice, she often agreed to stand in as goalie—without the benefit of gloves. She defended the goal as if her life were on the line, and left the field exhausted and bruised from shots that had ricocheted off every part of her body.

If we weren't playing sports, we were watching them. My parents were die-hard San Diego Padres fans, and when the ball games stretched past bedtime, Natalie and I would wake up to find sticky notes with the final score posted on our bed frames. I inherited that baseball DNA and idolized outfielder Tony Gwynn, the perennial All-Star who'd starred at San Diego State University and never never left the city. He was as much a part of my hometown as the beaches and the US Navy base.

As I got older, youth soccer became as much of a frustration as a passion. I was an instinctive forward, quick to the ball, but too slight to put enough punch into my shots and often overpowered one-on-one. If I didn't hold my own when things got physical, I'd be on the ground and soon on my way to warm the bench. "You have to play bigger than you are," coaches told me. "Believe you're bigger." It was my first taste of being labeled an underdog—a tiny finesse player battling it out among flying elbows and kicks to the shins, the one who didn't belong but was determined to make it work. That was hard enough, but what really bothered me was the political crap. You didn't have the newest shoes? See ya. Didn't live in the upscale La Jolla neighborhood? Take your ball to a different group. Mom wasn't willing to sleep with the coach? So long, starting lineup. The culture struck me as nuts.

I understood that competition was supposed to teach us how to succeed. I developed an early taste for success, but I resented my dad's compulsive, vicarious need for me to achieve, as if I couldn't be trusted to want it badly enough for myself. When the ball sailed into open space, I was expected to meet it perfectly every time, to avoid wasting the smallest opportunity. He hammered home his messages: "No shortcuts." "Nothing is given, everything is earned." "Do it twice, but the effort only counts once." All solid concepts, but the sense that he was in this with me was offset by continual reminders that I owed him for anything I accomplished. The better I did, the more indebted he made me feel. When he shelled out extra cash for a private lesson to shore up a weakness, he let me know how much it cost and how easily he could take it all away.

The only person who could fully appreciate what it felt like to walk that tightrope was my sister. Natalie and I were constantly managing how to reconcile our dad's good intentions, his desire for our lives to be better than his, with the way he came across. We navigated it differently. She was more willing to push back and battle it out verbally, while I tended to simmer and pick my spots. We each respected how the other one felt and traded off whose turn it was to take the heat, approaching it as teammates.

◆ ◆ ◆

I WAS TEN years old the spring morning my dad informed me that he'd signed me up for the Junior Carlsbad, a one-mile road race for kids held during the Carlsbad 5000 race weekend. It was an introduction to the sport at the annual event that also featured elite races and a community 5-kilometer run. I had never run just for the sake of running, but I wasn't intimidated. Racing hard to be first to the soccer ball came naturally to me; I was accustomed to dominating warm-up laps and fitness tests at soccer camps.

It was only when I arrived that I realized how out of place I was. *You can't see fitness, but you can dress the part,* I thought, and my black cotton sweatpants and sweatshirt were clearly wrong for the occasion. The kids in the front row of the pack were decked out in their tiny two-inch split running shorts and, even on this cool morning, a lightweight tank-top singlet. They rolled through a warm-up routine and got last-minute instructions from their coach. My dad's ritual was simpler. He told me to get right into that dressed-for-success pack and run hard.

As soon as the gun went off, fitting in no longer mattered. Breaking away from the crowd was the point, so I did. I was the top girl finisher by a large margin and beat most of the boys. Yet my biggest reward wasn't getting a medal or seeing a time on the clock—it was when my dad confirmed the otherness I'd felt at the start line. He loved that "we" had beat down the in-crowd. "Oh, man, that was great," he gushed. "You beat all those kids who are training for this. Look at them in all their fancy gear, and you just whooped up on them." The chip on my shoulder was definitely hereditary.

The only running I did for the next couple of years was to stay in shape for soccer and softball, but when I was in seventh grade, my dad, ever in search of opportunity, found a slot for me on the MLK Blasters youth track-and-field club, based at Morse High School. The Blasters, one of the top groups in Southern California, gave me a different taste of otherness. The team was entirely African American and entirely made up of sprinters, yet I felt embraced. Coach Adam Henderson had Monica, his daughter and assistant coach, put together my workouts—intervals on the track where I was alone other than the occasional presence of a local amateur runner named Doug. He was a slight Asian American guy in his forties who wore old-school split shorts and, impressed by what I was doing, told me more than once that I would go to the Olympics someday. I got used to the sound and feel of the cinders crunching under my feet, a tangible reminder that I was grinding away at getting better, and I loved the sensation of leaving Doug behind as we did our speed sessions. I thrived, winning races week after week in the San Diego youth division.

I competed in the 800-meter to 3,000-meter events most of the time, but on occasion, if a key athlete was injured or sick, I'd be chosen for the third leg of the 4×100-meter relay team. Normally, the unfamiliar pressure of running the 100 would have terrified me, but I knew we had the ultimate ringer on our anchor leg: Monique Henderson. Monica's little sister was my age but already setting records and showing signs of world-class talent. I could take the baton in first place, get crushed by the faster teams around me, and hand off to Monique in last place, yet she'd still pull off the win.

I liked that the clock didn't play favorites. Snotty kids and their overbearing parents couldn't influence what happened on the track. My hard work paid off in short order—I was almost immediately competitive in the youth ranks at the national level—and my steadily improving times became a source of both pride and slight anxiety for my mom and dad. They cheered me on and hoped running might help support my college education, but they didn't want the sport to propel me too far from home, even though that's exactly where my momentum was leading me. I felt an ownership over my results I hadn't felt in team sports, as if I were amassing evidence my dad couldn't dispute. I realized that running could be my ticket to escape his scrutiny, his temper, and ultimately, his home. Some of his values—his relentless work ethic, his insistence on doing things right, his disdain for shortcuts—were already deeply embedded in my psyche, but he lost his immediate leverage over me when I found my place in sport.

Running felt like independence. It gave me time that was completely within my control. I was in charge of how much effort I put in and what I took away. I could wrestle with daily problems in my high school world or tune them out and enjoy the scenery. I could run away from things I didn't want to confront or run straight toward a goal. Choosing to run was the first real decision I ever made. I ran because I wanted to, after years of playing other sports because I was told to. It put distance between who I was and who other people told me I should be.

◆ ◆ ◆

THE CHULA VISTA Olympic Training Center, nestled in the hills of a vast expanse of parkland just a few miles from my home, opened when I was twelve. At any given time, there were athletes from multiple Summer Olympic sports in residence, and I'd been there with my high school classes to watch field hockey and track workouts. I was enamored of the global spectacle and the intensity of the competition, especially in my now-chosen sport of track and field.

Michael Johnson and his golden shoes, flying to wins in the 200-meter and 400-meter events at the 1996 Summer Games in Atlanta, represented the epitome of excellence and cool to me.

As a high school junior, the idea of becoming an Olympian myself seemed simultaneously distant yet tangible. My club teammate Monique Henderson had been named to the Sydney 2000 US Olympic team when she was still in high school, and the mere fact that I'd been around an athlete who had reached that level at age seventeen made it seem like something real people could achieve. I jumped at the chance to take part in a youth camp at the OTC. It felt like a way to brush up against an ideal.

During a class session, we were asked to write our most treasured long-term running goal on a three-by-five-inch notecard. Frank Browne was sitting next to me—my third high school track coach in as many years, and by far my favorite. Frank was an English teacher at Hilltop High School in Chula Vista by day, and he had a way of making running cerebral yet fun, which was already pretty much my modus operandi in all things. We'd be studying training plans and race strategy one minute and then pivot to music and movies the next. I responded by buying into his coaching philosophy and quickly began notching personal bests.

Frank asked if he could peek at my notecard. I trusted him enough by that time to show him what I'd written: "Make an Olympic team." He didn't seem at all surprised or skeptical. "As long as you're enjoying yourself and having fun with this, you can go far in the sport," he said, words that hit home with me immediately. When the session ended, he started rattling off steps I would need to take to become an Olympian: first, improve my leg speed in the shorter distances; then shift to the 5,000- and 10,000-meter distances on the track; and ultimately, use the combination of speed and stamina to thrive in the marathon. It was the first time I ever heard my name and the word *marathon* mentioned in the same sentence. It didn't sound like an event I'd want to do. The marathon seemed like an activity to me, not a sport. It conjured up images of the times my parents took Natalie and me to the local track and joined other moms and dads with matching jogging suits, running lap after lap, thinking they were training for a "race." I couldn't see anything competitive about it.

Frank left Hilltop my senior year and began teaching at another San Diego school, but we continued working together with the blessing and help of the new coach. California Interscholastic Federation track-and-field competition was a true test of talent. There were no divisions between large and small high schools, public and private. Everyone was thrown into the same pool at county and sectional meets, and any runner who qualified for a CIF final probably could have been a state champion elsewhere. Thanks to a strong résumé of competitive times and respectable results at the state meets, I was recruited by dozens of universities and accepted a scholarship offer at Arizona State University—much to my parents' dismay. They had envisioned me joining Natalie at the University of California, Berkeley, where she was playing field hockey and happily immersed in her classes. Cal featured renowned academics, but just so-so cross-country and distance track programs at the time. Still, it was my first choice until I visited ASU, at Frank's suggestion, and sat across the desk from coach Walt Drenth.

Walt's office was filled with trophies and awards, but he hadn't been an instant success in Tempe. The year he arrived, the team had finished last at the Pacific-10 Conference championships. After that meet was over, he told me, a runner started bugging him about going to lunch. "We're not going to lunch," Walt said. "We're watching the awards, so you can see the winners get their trophy and understand how champions look and behave." His tone of voice was mild, but I could feel how forceful he would be when he needed to make a point. As we talked about his expectations for the team, I heard his passion for getting the absolute most out of people. He had a knack for taking decent-but-not-great athletes and catapulting them to the next level. ASU had surprised people by forging up near the top of the National Collegiate Athletic Association Division I heap, and Walt aspired to go further. He had a calm intensity about him, leavened with a low-key sense of humor. When I told him what I was planning to study, he told me not to pursue a degree in psychology. "I have one. It's not very practical," he said, then laughed at his own joke.

Meeting Walt made up my mind. I was drawn to his honesty and his standards. I could tell that running for him would shape me on and off the course. In his view, a champion's mentality was about far more than finishing first; he valued effort and mindset over outcome, although they often added up to the same thing. In my parents' eyes, I was choosing running over education. My rationale was that I could work hard at any school and make my education as useful and gratifying as I wanted it to be. I could seek out great programs, courses, and professors that would rival what I'd get at UC-Berkeley. I'll always remember my mom saying, "We're not mad. We're just disappointed." It bothered me. It also felt deeply fulfilling to chart my own path. I was very much the queen of *I'll show you*.

The one downside was that I wouldn't be sharing my college experience with Natalie. I was aware that I was opting out of what was comfortable and familiar, and that I'd miss her, but our bond was unbreakable. I would have stood in the way of an oncoming bus for her, and I knew she would have done the same for me.

◆ ◆ ◆

THE ARIZONA STATE team vibe proved to be reasonably in step with my own: a ragtag bunch relative to fearsome

Stanford University, the conference powerhouse with A-list recruits such as Sara Bei, Lauren Fleshman, Ryan Hall, Ian Dobson, and Alicia Craig. We never gave up on our conviction that we could beat them, but seldom did. In our defense, it took a unique degree of dedication to be a student-athlete at ASU, particularly as a distance runner logging hundreds of miles outdoors. The combination of ridiculous heat and a student body largely intent on getting shit-faced nightly from Wednesday through Saturday made for a potentially distracting environment. We had to be the only college kids in America begging our coach to push the 5:50 A.M. practices thirty minutes *earlier* so we could work out in cooler conditions. We'd roll into the track facility while most of Tempe slept, finish our sessions as campus began to stir, then brush off our work and blend into the crowd for the remainder of the day.

Amy Hastings arrived at ASU my sophomore year and became my usual training partner, even though we couldn't have been more different in many ways. She was blond and blue-eyed and Midwestern nice. She ran happy, not angry, and had a sort of endearing obliviousness that I used to tease her about. She was also stronger and faster than me, and training with her was a mixed blessing. We could handle the same total volume, and she helped motivate me to do seventy- to eighty-mile weeks, but I didn't put in the hours as consistently as she did. In track interval sessions—repeats of anywhere from two hundred meters to a mile—she could take me out of my comfort zone early. I'd overreach to try to hang on, and dig deeper with each successive rep. Our eight- to ten-mile tempo runs on Tempe's greenbelt played out the exact same way: I'd go out too hard, feel myself dying, fight to finish the workout, and then struggle to recover in the few days before the next hard effort. I was improving, but leaving my legs behind in workouts and showing up to races flat.

On Sunday mornings, we would head for South Mountain, where our typical route took us on a rugged uphill eight-mile trail and back again, baking in a landscape of red dirt and cacti. The experience was a living contradiction of hell and sanctuary: the Church of the Sunday Long Run. There was something soothing and near sacred about putting in mile after mile, stockpiling work into a fitness bank, chiseling away weak parts of body and mind. When we left for those runs, it wasn't uncommon to see students stumbling back from the evening before. We played a fun people-watching game—"heading home or going out?"—that was not hard to win. Seeing evidence of the excesses of campus life at dawn was a reminder of an alternate scenario we could have chosen, but our sense of time well spent usually blotted out any pangs.

We were well aware of excess on the other end of the spectrum, where athletes took discipline to an unhealthy extreme. NCAA Division I women's track culture was clearly struggling with a stick-figure body image ideal. Looking around at meets, we had no trouble picking out the runners who were limiting their daily intake to a few apple slices or sticking their fingers down their throats after over-indulging. The problem was that a lot of those runners were also consistently performing well. To me, it seemed as if dis-ordered eating and unnaturally light physiques on women's teams were viewed as a necessary passage, something you did if you were "serious." As long as they were getting re-sults, the sport looked the other way and ignored the long-term sickness it could create.

I couldn't accept that as the price for success in college or at any level, and Amy felt the same way. Running was just running, not a reason to manipulate our entire beings. I wasn't as stick-thin as I'd been in high school, but I knew that was supposed to happen as I matured. I didn't care what people thought of the way I looked or whether it matched some insanely gaunt archetype. My dad had been vehement about food as necessary fuel for sport, which had led to my somewhat matter-of-fact attitude about it. But even though I was hardly a gourmet, I knew that depriving myself would make a fun pursuit more like an obligation. Amy and I talked about it a lot. She tackled the problem by putting in the same degree of effort year-round. I never had to worry about following any particular diet or counting calories. I ate until I was full and then stopped, and I was judicious about alcohol consumption during the track and cross-country seasons. That was the limit of what I was willing to do. I didn't go off the rails the rest of the year, but I gave myself a break. There is a reason it's called the off-season.

I wasn't about to starve myself of experiences, either. My teammates Cody Sohn and Megan Laib loved indie rock as much as I did, and we gravitated to concerts where we knew we'd be among plenty of like-minded outsiders. There was nothing better than hearing Saves the Day belt out the soundtrack of our youth from the crush of the mosh pit, where strangers trusted other strangers to hoist each other aloft and float them through the crowd, riding the currents of the music and staring at the sky.

And sail, belly up to the clouds
The rocks scraping our backs
To breathe in the air will be
The only thing that we have

They literally had my back, and I had theirs. There was no right or wrong look to fit in. Nobody questioned how seriously I took the music and if that made me a "real" fan or not.

So many of my best moments at ASU were far removed

from racing and helped me understand what really sustained me. My friendship with Amy was something I especially appreciated in real time. It always seemed easy, no matter how our athletic lives were going; we were compatible enough to room together at away meets. We shared countless laughs at the world's absurdity and hundreds of stories about family, classes, and running dreams and goals, but we could tick off miles in total silence, too, never needing to fill the void with noise. After finishing off a long run covered in sweat, salt, and red Arizona dust, there was always a feeling that we had gotten better that day. Amy pushed me a little beyond what I thought was possible, and hopefully the reverse was true. This balancing act of ours—running and studying, camaraderie and competition, excellence and moderation—demanded a lot from us, and yet it felt as if we didn't have a care in the world.

◆   ◆   ◆

WALT TOOK THE head cross-country and track coaching job at Michigan State University before my senior year. I could adjust to a coaching change—I'd had so many in high school—but the season deteriorated for another reason when I developed plantar fasciitis, the most persistent and troublesome injury I'd had up to that point. It afflicts connective tissue in the foot and its cause is somewhat of a medical mystery, but there was nothing mysterious about the symptoms. I felt as if one of my shoes were filled with shards of glass that I was crushing with every step. The sensation was worst in the early miles of a run, until I warmed up and was able to go hard enough to reaggravate it all over again. I still managed to qualify through regionals for the 5,000-meter event at the NCAA championships. The meet happened to be in Sacramento that year, but it didn't promise to be much of a celebratory trip to my home state. As I lined up for my semifinal heat, I knew I would be going through the motions. No warm-up or race-day adrenaline was going to dull the pain enough to allow me to perform respectably. I suffered on every lap and finished dead last in an ugly seventeen minutes plus—an anticlimactic bookend to my collegiate career. On one hand, it was a sign that my body had been through enough, and it was time to move on. Yet it left me with curiosity about what I could do if I were a hundred percent healthy and devoted fully to the task.

I'd chosen ASU based on my instinct about Walt and the program, but I had always considered myself a student-athlete, in that order. As a student, I'd done what I set out to do: I was graduating with bachelor's degrees in psychology and religious studies. I had taken running seriously, but never nurtured any athletic ambitions beyond college. By contrast, Amy had dreamed bigger. She had envisioned herself turning pro and treated running as if it were already a full-time job, an investment I admired but resisted, as much as I loved the sport. She adapted to more aggressive training, improved steadily, set school records, and made herself into one of the premier distance athletes in the Pac-10. I had relied on my natural talent and an on-again, off-again work ethic that, predictably, yielded decent results interspersed with glimmers of brilliance. I was a two-time All-American, but never put together that singular meaningful performance or generated the buzz that would have landed me a big pro contract. I kept circling back to the thought that I'd run my personal best in the 5,000 the very first time I tried the event as a sophomore, then stagnated. I knew I had room to grow.

◆ ◆ ◆

As uncertainty about my future loomed larger in my mind, there was one thing I knew I'd been right about: Working with Walt had made me mentally tougher and given me valuable life tools. He shaped the way I looked at adversity—as a puzzle or a challenge instead of a hardship, something to be approached with logic rather than emotion. Now I was graduating with no plan and nothing to guide me except that logic and a still-nebulous belief that I'd figure it out.

We'd stayed in touch, and at the Stanford Invitational meet in March 2005, Walt introduced me to Keith and

Kevin Hanson. Kevin, who had been Walt's teammate at Central Michigan University, and his brother had started a new residential training group backed by the Brooks Running company in an unlikely locale: suburban Rochester Hills, thirty miles north of Detroit. They called their team the Original Distance Project (ODP) and stocked it with underdogs from smaller colleges and a few from big programs who aspired to get better. From afar, I had the impression that it was a group where everyone ran with something to prove. It sounded like the kind of atmosphere I needed while I figured out whether I could commit to a more focused running lifestyle.

I reached out to the Hansons early that summer to see if they'd take me on. Over the phone and in emails, they did their best to dissuade me, warning that Michigan winters would be tough on someone from Southern California via Arizona. That just made me dig in. I told them that running in stifling heat was great practice for managing extreme discomfort. They relented and invited me for a visit.

When I sat down with Kevin and Keith in their office, they read my draft contract aloud, line by line, including every potential payoff from the bonus sheet. It was all new to me and made me feel like a kid being talked at, but it also drove home the massive opportunity on the table. I didn't have multiple offers to put side by side and an agent to guide me through the process. This was my only option, and I knew I was fortunate to have it. My dad's credo scrolled through my head. *"Find opportunities wherever you can, and when you do find them, don't squander them."* I remembered Frank's faith in me and Walt's long-game philosophy that effort was always worthwhile even when the outcome wasn't predictable.

I had toyed with going to grad school and kicking the can down the road in academia as a lifelong student or a professor, but I'd taken no actual steps in that direction, which told me that I was being tugged toward something else. There was no way to know how much better I could be as an athlete unless I gave myself more time. I didn't want to be haunted years down the line by what-ifs, and the only way to avoid that was to chase down an answer, whether I liked that answer or not.

◆　◆　◆

I TRAVELED LIGHT when I lifted off from San Diego a few weeks later: two checked bags and a backpack. The rest of my cargo—my parents' precepts, my coaches' teachings, my sister's unwavering support—was invisible. There was a lot I didn't know about where I was going, but I was sure I needed to seek out my own place and pace.

Natalie's steadfast self-belief was a big reason I was on the plane; her example had given me the final impetus I needed. Her bank account balance had been close to zero when she graduated from Berkeley with a communications degree, but she was intent on living in one of the most expensive cities in the world: San Francisco. I thought she was attempting the impossible and that she'd be moving back home soon enough, but she landed a job in finance, packed her bags, and dismissed how crazy it looked from the outside. Now she was killing it. If she could be that gutsy, so could I. It made the notion of moving more than two thousand miles away to Michigan much more appealing—and valid.

As I settled into my window seat, my mind drifted back to the week I'd recently spent with Natalie in Manhattan, where her company had sent her for the summer. I'd never been to New York, and her invitation was a welcome graduation gift. We shared her room at the upscale Le Parker Meridien and played tourist, walking for miles, hitting the Metropolitan Museum of Art and Times Square, staying up until all hours to take full advantage of the city's nightlife.

I hadn't been running much, giving myself a break before I dove into a more intense lifestyle, but the rolling green oasis of Central Park beckoned from just a couple of blocks away, and I made an exception to lace up with Natalie. Sharing a few miles on those paths that serve as a training ground for both the mediocre and the mighty was one more way of savoring our time together. It was definitely a passage—a more significant one than deciding to go to a different school. We would be farther apart than we'd ever been in our lives. I knew our loyalty to each other would be a permanent part of my inner landscape, unlike the outline of the Southern California coast, already blurred and falling away behind me as the plane banked to the east.

MILE ZERO

THE BUS RIDE to the start in Hopkinton typically takes about fifty minutes. As many times as I've made the trip—this will be the sixth—I'm always daunted by the idea that I'm expected to run all the way back. That's even more true this time, with the fearsome weather pounding away outside. It's simultaneously twisted and brilliant that a storm will provide perfect cover for me today. I can preserve my fatigued body and buy time to get a handle on my health situation. The weather is a tangible asset for me and a glimmer of hope that has been rare this race weekend.

I climb onto my assigned bus and immediately begin scanning faces, looking for one man in particular. I don't see him, so I grab a seat in the third row, just ahead of Shalane Flanagan, the reigning New York City Marathon champion and an Olympic teammate of mine at the 2012 and 2016 Summer Games. She's leaning in, chatting with her coach, Jerry Schumacher. I hope they have the winning formula today. Shalane and I have nearly zero in common beyond our love of hammering our bodies—and competitors—into the ground over long distances, but we've built a strong mutual respect over the years as our rivalry has played out on the roads. That regard deepened as we both spoke out about wanting a clean sport and level playing field, topics most athletes are afraid to take on. I'd like to see her win on this course, in her hometown. The women's field is stacked with American talent. If we can't do it this year, the future looks dismal. We share a quick smile and a friendly nod before I hunker down in my seat.

As athletes and support crew members continue to file onto the bus, my expression says, *Don't even think about sitting in the empty seat next to me.* Ordinarily, that seat would be filled by one of my coaches, but not today. In fact, I'm very confident that my coaches for most of the last thirteen years will be actively rooting against me. It's hard to say for certain, since we've conversed only two or three times over the last nine months, and the last forty-eight hours certainly haven't strengthened our relationship.

Then I see a head of familiar curly hair, followed by the boyish face of John Ball. He's the guy I'm looking for. John is officially licensed as a chiropractor, but only because they don't give out licenses for miracle workers. John's spot-on gait analysis, therapeutic massage, and adjustments have saved more than a few prominent athletes from having to end careers prematurely. I've been a client since 2012, when he rehabilitated me after a fractured femur. He's become an integral part of my team since then, and there's nobody I trust more when making career decisions based on my health. We've been planning for this day since early February, and I trusted him when we decided that there was no magical fix for me in this race. I would do my best to look like the athlete I've always been, then consider stepping off the course at some point in the second half of the race to save my body for other fights on other days. It could be risky to do anything else. But that plan is now in flux for a couple of reasons.

I give him a quick wave. My eyes say, *You're sitting here.*

John lowers himself next to me. We share a wordless, telepathic look: *The torrential downpour is the best thing that could have happened today, and it's going to change everything.*

I lean toward John and whisper, "Do you think I can finish today?"

He raises his eyebrows and smirks slightly. "If it goes out slow enough, yeah," he says. His face gets serious, and he lowers his voice. "When the gun goes off, it's going to be a fight to get to the back of the pack. Just take it mile by mile. If you think you're doing long-term damage, just step off."

"I think I can finish."

"I think you can, too."

We both have to suppress giddy laughter.

The sirens of the motorcade's police escort begin to wail, and red and blue lights whirl in the dank garage. As the buses roll out, we get our first real glimpse of the storm. Rain lashes against the windows, and gale-force winds whip sheets of water across the sky and over the road. We'll be fighting a headwind for the entire 26.2 miles on the point-to-point course. The friendly chatter that had filled the bus moments earlier dies instantly, and tension takes its place. I can see it written on runners' faces and in their jittery legs and feet. It feels suffocating. The Boston Marathon is tough enough, with its tactical, hilly terrain. There's no crutch in the form of a designated pacesetter out front, as there is at the London Marathon and other major races. The extreme conditions will add an unexpected degree of difficulty.

Suddenly, I'm immune to the cloud of anxiety. This situation is strangely soothing for me, and I feel a sense of ease and calm. John sees it in my eyes and my demeanor, and he relaxes, too. I grab my phone, slide on my headphones, and turn my Spotify to Johnny Cash's "God's Gonna Cut You Down." The rhythmic thumping of the tune and the gravelly voice of the Man in Black pair perfectly with my mood. It's become a tradition for me to post a prerace tweet with the lyrics that speak to me in the moment. So I do:

Well, you may throw your rock and hide your hand
Workin' in the dark against your fellow man

But as sure as God made black and white
What's down in the dark will be brought to the light

You can run on for a long time
Run on for a long time
Run on for a long time
Sooner or later God'll cut you down
#TogetherForward

◆ ◆ ◆

THE KOREAN PRESBYTERIAN church in Hopkinton is a place of reverence in a different way every third Monday in April, by virtue of its location: steps from the start line. About a hundred of us in the elite field stream out of the buses and hustle through the downpour to a back entrance, heads bent down, shielding our faces from the rain. A row of portable toilets stands against the blank white canvas that is the back of the church; either a running event is about to take place, or this is the home of the worst buffet ever. We hustle into a large, open room with a white linoleum floor, looking for a good spot to land. Sleeping pads are laid out around the perimeter and child-sized chairs sit scattered randomly in the middle. Some groups head for the children's classrooms. The place reeks of age, worship, and, now, sweat and anxiety. We'll spend the next ninety minutes here.

Selecting gear to run for two and a half hours with temperatures in the thirties, heavy rain, and a twenty- to thirty-mile-per-hour headwind most of the way is a challenge. What I choose could help or haunt me. If I dress too heavily, I'll be tempted to shed layers too early in the race—I know the weather always gets colder and windier as we go along. If I dress too lightly, I might never warm up. If I burn through glycogen—the stored form of glucose, which fuels the body—too soon, I could slow down to the point where my body temperature could drop dangerously low, bringing on hypothermia.

The energy inside the building is chaotic. People head out to do a quick warm-up jog and return soaking wet, seeking out a physio or grabbing a coach for one last game-plan chat. No one wants to fuck up three months of work with a dumb race decision. They're timing their last toilet pit stops, searching for safety pins for race bibs, doing drills and stretches. Nobody wants to spend any more time than necessary outside in the elements today. John checks on me once or twice, making sure I don't need any last-minute adjustments or general comforting.

After some thought, I place my race bib number sideways on my running jacket, where it won't get caught in the zipper or impede my arm swing. That will make it easier to peel off the jacket later, although I doubt I'll still be on the course at the point where I would consider it. Underneath the jacket, pinned to my jersey, is the second, official race bib. It's unlikely anyone will see it today.

Mary Kate Shea, the elite athlete coordinator for principal sponsor John Hancock, takes attendance so she can line us up in race bib numerical order—a roll call that provides comic relief every year. Everyone has some last-minute thing to do, nobody is ever ready when she calls their name, and, once she gets them in line, no one stays in place. Truly like herding cats. It's a clown show to me, but not so much for MK. We're good friends, I'm familiar with her responsibilities, and I know she has a very specific broadcast deadline for getting us to the start. I've developed a humorous routine with her over the years: If MK calls a name and the person doesn't show right away, I tell her she needs to scratch them because they clearly don't want to race.

"Edna Kiplagat. Edna, are you here? Edna."

Edna is bib 1, the defending champion, and also, in my opinion, the greatest female marathoner in the world over the last decade. She won Boston 2017 in absolutely dominating fashion. Her legs and lungs go on forever and she has a super-savvy racing mind. There's no part of Edna that isn't made for going fast, and she's also sturdy and strong enough for the Boston course, a relatively rare combination.

Her Kenyan compatriot Gladys Chesir, who's wearing bib 12 today, ran a strong 2 hours, 24 minutes, and

51 seconds for a personal best time last year on the flat roads of Amsterdam. Her Boston debut a year ago didn't go as well, as she fell far behind the leaders' pace and finished a distant fifth behind my fourth place, minutes slower than what she's capable of. That's all I know about Chesir, except that experience matters so much here, and she may be better on her second attempt.

"Bib 5: Shalane. Where's Shalane?"

Shalane Flanagan is the first US woman to win in New York in forty years. Incredible for her, incredible for our generation after years of people asking why American women's distance running had tanked. Yet I suspect if you asked her which race she'd give an arm to win, it would be Boston—the race that she'd watched goggle-eyed as a kid growing up nearby in the North Shore town of Marblehead.

"Bib 8: Des."

I'm behind Mamitu Daska, an Ethiopian who ran third in New York City last year. I expect her to push the pace early. A couple of other top Americans are called after me: Serena Burla and Molly Huddle. Most followers of the sport view Molly as the next breakthrough US marathoner. There is one top-ten bib missing, however: Jordan Hasay, who had scratched the night before with an injured heel. Jordan has been a superstar since high school—the Nike prodigy of the moment who finished third here last year—but I don't expect her absence to alter the dynamics of the race.

On paper, there's still a legit chance for us to end the

American drought we're all so tired of hearing about, a losing streak in Boston that dates back thirty-three years. Lisa Larsen Weidenbach's win in 1985 came before prize money revolutionized the women's side of the sport and East Africans flooded major marathon fields. There were a lot of theories about why we hadn't been able to keep up, but this fact was indisputable: Only a handful of US athletes had come close to crashing the recent Kenyan-Ethiopian dominance in Boston. I was one of them, but that was seven years ago now. People had gotten used to seeing me in the hunt but not quite able to close it out.

We parade into the holding area—a soggy, low-key procession, under the circumstances. There will be no reprieve from the conditions for a long time now. It's as ugly as I imagined. The skies are low and dark, the downpour shows no signs of letting up, and fans are sparse. It's weird not hearing and feeling that typical rowdy energy from crowds massed along the barriers. We have ten minutes to jog on the first four hundred meters of the course. I'm wearing a new model of shoes I got six days ago—something I wouldn't normally risk, but I'm gambling that it won't matter today. I test my soles on the painted lines to see if they're slippery. All good, but footing is treacherous on a couple of slick manhole covers. That will be another trap on the road.

When we're lined up at the start and the TV cameras are panning down the row, I take a minute to scan the faces around me. All I see are expressions of absolute misery, and the gun hasn't even gone off yet. No one looks mentally ready for this. Someone will wear the champion's olive branch wreath in three hours, but if I'm reading minds correctly, most of my competitors are thinking about self-preservation, not glory. And what does my face give away to them? Nothing, I hope. I feel myself smiling at the bizarre dichotomy: the worst weather I've ever raced in; the best thing that could have happened to me.

Just past nine-thirty in the morning, the official starter yells, "One minute to race time!" The next sixty seconds feel elastic and endless, the prelude to a couple of hours that usually flash by.

Thirty seconds.

I pitch the knit winter hat I'm wearing and replace it with a dry headband.

Twenty seconds.

We're all doing nervous jumps and useless stretches.

Ten seconds.

I reflexively crouch into a race stance: left foot with toes immediately behind the start line, right foot a step back, primed for a quick push off the ground. My index finger hovers over the start button of my GPS watch. Everything is aligned to blast forward at the crack of the gun.

Five seconds.

I think of what John told me on the bus: When the gun goes off, the goal is going to be to hide from the elements as quickly as possible.

Four . . .

I straighten up, backing off my aggressive crouch, remembering I'm not in a hurry today.

Three . . . two . . . one.

Bang!

INVESTMENT

APRIL TURNED UGLY in southeastern Michigan the day that Dick Beardsley joined the Hansons-Brooks women's team for an easy six-mile run. We stepped out of our group house in Rochester Hills at seven-thirty in the morning and found the roads slicked by temperatures in the low twenties, so we stuck to the sidewalks, trying to avoid icy patches. Understandably, most of my training partners just wanted to get out of the wind and cold, and they dropped Beardsley in a hurry. I loitered behind, going super-easy, taking advantage of the chance to chat him up about the race that had defined his career.

Beardsley knew more than most about running in less than ideal weather. He had waged one of the great Boston Marathon battles of all time with Alberto Salazar in 1982 on a course baking in eighty-degree temperatures. A quarter century later, that race remained compelling enough to have become the basis for a book by sportswriter John Brant, *Duel in the Sun,* which Beardsley was in town to promote. He rattled off Boston landmarks that were still vivid to him, each one with a backstory: Lake Cochituate in Natick, where, legend had it, 1936 champion Ellison "Tarzan" Brown jumped in to cool off during the race; Heartbreak Hill, named for Johnny Kelley's anguish when Brown dropped him there; the spot in Brookline where, in 1979, twenty-one-year-old Joan Benoit grabbed a Boston Red Sox hat from a friend, put it on backward, and wore it the rest of the way as a reminder not to blow a sure lead the year after her favorite team had collapsed to the hated New York Yankees.

Salazar held the marathon world record back then, while Beardsley was an accomplished but largely unknown athlete in a sport that was still early in its evolution from fringe pastime to major industry. The two of them had broken away in the last nine miles and repeatedly traded leads, duking it out all the way to the homestretch on Boylston Street. It was fascinating to hear Beardsley describe digging in, his legs all but numb, and feeling his hamstring seize up—only to have it unkink again when he stepped into a pothole. By then, Salazar had mustered a final kick to win by two seconds. Both men finished under 2:09, breaking the existing American record and creating an instant classic. At a time when just a handful of pro runners could make a real living, Beardsley understood that only one man would reap the benefits. Winning would have changed his life. Instead, he went back to his farm in Minnesota.

I had more than a passing interest in listening to Beardsley break down the hills and straightaways of the course, the thrill of running through the crowds pressing against the barricades. I was a student taking mental notes in a private seminar, ten days out from my own marathon debut at Boston 2007. I wanted to know everything I could about what I was in for. And I loved the image of the lesser-known runner pushing a favorite, defying the conditions, surprising everyone.

◆　◆　◆

CLUB-BASED DISTANCE TRAINING groups began springing up in the United States during the running boom in the 1970s and 1980s, died back, and began to reappear again in the early 2000s after a prolonged slump by American runners. Regional groups—Team USA Minnesota, Team USA California, Team USA Monterey Bay—were formed to get the United States back in competitive shape. The Mammoth Track Club (originally Team Running USA), where Terrence Mahon coached Deena Kastor and rising talent Ryan Hall, had marathon star power that included Deena's fellow 2004 Olympic marathon medalist Meb Keflezighi. When I graduated from ASU in 2005, the preeminent group on the track was Alberto Salazar's Nike Oregon Project, based at

Nike's corporate headquarters in Beaverton. Kara Goucher, an NCAA track and cross-country champion from the University of Colorado, had signed there the year before and was gaining ground in the pro ranks.

I had limited knowledge about those programs or the running industry in general when I migrated to one of the most untraditional training bases in the country. Kevin and his younger brother, Keith, formed the Hansons Original Distance Project in 1999 as an alternative for runners like me who came out of college with unfulfilled promise and a résumé not quite shiny enough to attract big sponsorship. The brothers wanted to create an environment where athletes could build fitness and aim for slow, steady development as they worked their way up. Brooks, their shoe sponsor, was a solid company with credibility in the sport but still a relative upstart in elite running compared with Nike and Adidas.

My one-year contract—as with all the Hansons' athlete contracts—spelled out a bonus-only structure, which rewarded success. One hundred percent of my earnings would go straight into my pocket, a huge upside for me as I started out—but this also meant no guaranteed income if I were to get injured or have a tough spell. The brothers, in turn, had a contract with Brooks that provided our budget for travel, physio services, and other expenses. They waived the standard fifteen percent agents' cut for runners who opted to be represented by them—a practical option for those of us who were scrapping to make it. The Hansons also provided jobs for some athletes at their four Hansons Running Shops in the Detroit area, where we all got stipends to spend on Brooks gear.

We could choose to live cheaply in one of three houses owned by the program. It was like an extension of college with a bit more pocket change; a basic existence that definitely provided motivation to climb the ladder. My bedroom in the ranch house on Tienken Road had a leaky window that left my comforter soaked any time it rained, and on one morning, we gathered in the living room before a run and were greeted by a gaping hole above us and soggy rot on the floor. We pooled our resources for meals and ate family style. Melissa White and Chad Johnson were always kind enough to include me in whatever they were pulling together for dinner, and I'd chip in with ingredients or cash. Chad's favorite, macaroni and cheese with scrambled eggs, was surprisingly good. The overall arrangement seemed simple and sensible to me: Work hard, perform well, get paid.

Kevin did the bulk of the coaching, wrote the workouts, and usually carried the most weight when it came to setting race schedules. Keith assisted at training sessions by reading splits, shouting encouragement, and handing out water bottles, but his role was chiefly on the financial side, managing the running shops and the business end of the team. They often finished each other's sentences, but the brothers had very different personalities. Kevin was intense, extroverted, emotionally invested in his runners, and a perfectionist when it came to race plans and preparation—the guy who would stay up all night trying to get a detail exactly right. Keith struck me as more easygoing and relaxed, someone who separated his job from his identity.

I showed up super out of shape after a summer of relative leisure. Within a few months of trying to play catch-up, I was nursing a stress fracture in my right foot, the first injury that had sidelined me for an extended period of time. I had to rebuild slowly, and I was in a good place to do that. The team dynamic was all about parity and camaraderie; we were going to be late bloomers if we were going to bloom at all. Two of my regular training partners were making the transition to road racing. Melissa had walked onto a Division III team at the State University College of New York at Geneseo, while Dot McMahan, a few years older than me, had been an 800 specialist at the University of Wisconsin–Milwaukee. On the men's side, Brian Sell was making a name for himself. At the 2004 US Olympic trials, his second marathon, he led through Mile 21 before hitting the wall and finishing thirteenth. Watching his dream slip away in those last few miles was the only push he needed for the next four years. In 2006, my first full year at Hansons, he broke out with a win at the National Half Marathon Championships and finished fourth in Boston with a personal best of 2:10:55.

Kevin structured marathon training blocks around a

philosophy of "running tired": ramping up volume to repli-
cate the fatigue that would set in after twenty miles, extend-
ing that plateau with quality workouts while legs were heavy
all the way up to race week, and skipping a conventional
chunk of recovery. Brian thrived on that regimen, putting
in as much as 160 miles a week during his marathon builds
even as he regularly declared he was ready to retire and apply to dental school. His commitment in the moment was
obvious, and we were all encouraged to follow his work-
horse ethic.

There were no jobs open at the Hansons' running shops
when I arrived, so I found one at a local outdoor gear store,
Moosejaw Mountaineering: four six-hour shifts a week at
minimum wage, taking customer service calls and emails.
The store managers understood my day job as a runner, and
they were incredibly accommodating about my schedule,
but when the holidays came around, I had to pull the same
all-nighters as everyone else. I dealt with a crazy workload
on those graveyard shifts that ended at five in the morning—
two-hundred-plus orders to handle compared with fifty on
a typical day, and hundreds more stacked up in my inbox—
but I looked forward to that time of the year. The store had
a fun, laid-back vibe, and when the pace ratcheted up, so
did the irreverent spirit. There was always good music
cranked on the speakers, office dogs lounging around, a
Ping-Pong table ready for action, and an occasional in-house
Friday happy hour. We were all in the shitstorm together.

Having a social life apart from running was absolutely key to my mental health. People at Moosejaw knew and admired what I did but weren't overly awed by it. When I missed a big running goal, they tended to see how much I'd achieved rather than where I'd fallen short: "Cool, good job, here's some orders for the day." It put the right level of importance on running. I was committed to figuring out who I could be as an athlete, but I knew myself well enough to understand that I couldn't obsess about it every waking minute.

◆ ◆ ◆

THE HANSONS SPECIALIZED in coaching the marathon, and my high school coach Frank Browne had pitched it to me years before as my path to the Olympics. I still thought the idea sounded horrible and had an attitude about it that bordered on disdain. Sure, I'd been pumped watching Deena at the 2004 Olympics. But for me, the idea of going that far made me feel as if I'd be running for the sake of running, not really testing how fast I was. I envisioned myself staying on the track and mastering the 5,000 and the 10,000, distances where I was sure I could be much better if I focused. In my mind, they were sexier events, all about putting my hand in the fire and holding it there as long as I could—a pure physical test with no patience involved, torturous but thrilling. And yet I was making decent progress in the longer distances. I made the US team for the

2006 World Road Running Championships in Debrecen, Hungary, and ran the 20-kilometer event in 1:11:56—a pretty successful day for me.

The first time I really understood the aura of the marathon was as an interested spectator at the finish line of the 2006 Chicago Marathon. Kevin had arranged a volunteer position for me, and I worked as a gofer in the elite suite for a couple of days leading up to the race, filling snack bowls, topping off refreshments, and making sure agents, coaches, and athletes were comfortable. On race day itself, I was stationed just beyond the finish line, handing out towels and directing or assisting runners to the elite recovery tent.

It was raining on and off as two Kenyan men, Robert Cheruiyot and Daniel Njenga, dueled through the last mile, both looking completely gassed as they willed their bodies to respond. Every time Cheruiyot opened up a little space, Njenga slammed it shut, refusing to give in. As Cheruiyot approached the finish banner with a small gap, he raised his hands in celebration, slipped on the painted logo just shy of the timing mat, and fell on his back, hitting his head hard. He left in a wheelchair, the winner by five seconds. I contemplated how miserable it would be to run my ass off for 26.1 miles, then have to dig even deeper and summon another gear. My legs hurt just thinking about it.

My respect for the event grew exponentially as I saw how drained, yet gratified, runners looked at the finish. I was able to see how the activity and the sport—masses and elites running on the same course on the same day—coexisted and complemented one another. The professionals at the front were testing their athletic boundaries; I'd been wrong to think they'd merely lost a step on the track and were headed out to pasture. Likewise, the amateurs straggling over the finish line hours later—whom I'd foolishly viewed as running for the sake of running—were working every bit as hard, digging deep and finding out what they were made of. Some looked strong and powerful, as if they'd conquered a beast. Others were glassy-eyed with miscalculation and defeat.

My teammates Melissa and Dot, in their passages from distance runners to marathoners, had very different days. Melissa had been flawless in training but went out too fast, hit the wall hard, struggled after the halfway point, and finished sixteenth. Dot came in twenty-third, yet closed really well and looked like she had more left in her. Knowing what their race plans had been going in, watching them execute, and seeing their respective outcomes told the story of how tough it was to get everything exactly right on race day. Unlike the track, where you could usually out-grit poor decisions, mistakes were magnified over 26.2 miles. What was it like to make those calculations in real time? I was intrigued.

Why not me? I couldn't come up with a good enough answer, so I decided to get out of my own way and open myself to possibility. When I asked the Hansons if I could finally try the marathon, they laughed, understandably—that's where they'd always wanted to steer me. Deciding where I would debut was easy. Boston would be hosting the 2008 US women's Olympic marathon team trials on a slightly different course from the traditional point-to-point: a loop that toured downtown, starting and finishing on Boylston Street. Being there a year before was the best way for me to prepare. We could double up on course tours and get a feel for the logistics and the energy of race weekend.

The marathon had an unmistakable emotional pull, but I viewed my choice as pragmatic, not romantic. Road racing was potentially more lucrative. The masses paid part of the freight for those events. Along with corporate sponsorships, they made it possible for organizers to offer hefty appearance fees and prize money. By contrast, track pros were limited to smaller fields in the few meets that mattered. All but a handful struggled to earn a living, and those at the very top squeezed everything they could from it before transitioning to the road. I wasn't going to chip away at being a professional runner indefinitely and go into debt doing it. I had given myself a one- to two-year window to measure my progress and see whether I had a prayer of making a living. In the cold light of day, that wouldn't be enough time to get me where I aspired to be on the track. I didn't want to settle for being one of the top Americans. To make all this work worthwhile and justify staying in the sport, I wanted to make an Olympic team. I knew I could qualify for Olympic trials on the road, and there was a gaping hole in American talent in the event. It was unusual at that time to launch a marathon career at age twenty-three, but I saw the opportunity in it. This would be my equivalent of buckling down and seeing if I could get my own start-up off the ground.

◆ ◆ ◆

INTRIGUING PROSPECTS OF a different kind propelled me forward as I trained for my marathon debut, in the form of Ryan Linden, a local runner who occasionally worked out with the ODP. Ryan owned a small landscaping company and lived on Thalia Avenue, near our house on Tienken. He had a mop of dark, curly hair, muttonchop sideburns, expressive eyes that always seemed to be smiling, and a strong chin with a distinctive dimple. He'd been a swimmer and a runner in high school and harbored hopes of making the track team at Michigan State University, but when he found out there were no walk-ons allowed, he began training for marathons—at age eighteen.

Our first interaction, not long after I moved to Michigan, was the opposite of auspicious. Ryan, a huge sports fan with a head for detail, followed the MSU track program closely and started a conversation about the women's collegiate scene. When he seemed underwhelmed by my résumé, I pushed back: "I was in the national meet a couple times. I'm not that bad."

"Can't pretty much anybody get to nationals out of the west region?" he said.

I thought he was a condescending jerk. He thought I was arrogant and didn't have the talent to back it up. But as we kept crossing paths over the next couple of years, something more sparked from that initial friction, and we began to date, casually at first. By the spring of 2007, for the first time since I had arrived in Michigan, I didn't feel isolated and transient. I looked forward to being around him. A three-month training block no longer seemed like an eternity.

Ryan witnessed one of my first real efforts to stand up for myself with the Hansons. We were gathered at a boat launch in Stony Creek Metropark, the start-finish point for most of our workouts, after one of our last pre-Boston sessions. I was livid, convinced that Kevin and Keith were holding me back, and ready to express that out loud. They wanted me to play it safe, guarantee a positive experience, and shoot for a 6:17-per-mile average pace and a 2:45 finish, two minutes faster than what I needed to qualify for the 2008 Olympic trials.

My ambition was running hot now that I was deeply invested in marathon training. I argued that I should be aiming higher. I had taken to the volume naturally; 115-mile weeks had begun to feel routine, a source of strength rather than sheer fatigue. It was a big jump after topping out at 80-mile weeks in college, but respect for the distance and fear of the unknown had forced me to dedicate myself. I was getting better with each workout and had come to love that feeling of stacking up days and weeks with a singular purpose. Front-loading all the pressure on one day—or maybe, in the future, a couple of marathons a year—narrowed the chance to excel and raised the stakes in a way I relished. Some of my teammates were chasing a 2:39 time goal, and I was holding my own in training with them. I had finally put in the work, and I wanted a payoff. Even in my debut, I didn't want to go to Boston and run just okay.

Ryan watched from afar as I made my case, wondering how much I'd push the brothers, admiring my passion. Afterward, privately, he seconded my growing self-belief. I didn't know it at the time, but I had just gained another important member of my permanent support crew. I was going to need that unconditional backing, because the Boston Marathon was about to change the trajectory of my life.

◆ ◆ ◆

I BEGAN TO bond with Boston on my first course tour, which included an introduction to Gloria Ratti, the first lady of the Boston Athletic Association. She and director of communications Jack Fleming greeted me and my Hansons-Brooks teammates as if we were VIPs rather than first-timers. I loved Gloria from the jump. Dressed impeccably in her blue BAA blazer, a silk scarf knotted around her neck with the sure touch of a fashion maven, she made my name a jovial exclamation: *"DAY-suh-ray!"* Her throaty voice was layered with warmth and authority.

Gloria, who spent four decades working for the US Central Intelligence Agency, started out as a race volunteer in the 1960s and played a huge role in growing the women's side of the race. It was also Gloria who advanced the idea of keeping records for all finishers and awarding medals to the masses. She became the first woman to serve on the BAA's board of governors, but her true love was her job as race historian. That was obvious as she and Jack led us through the displays of bibs, shoes, trophies, photographs, and other memorabilia that she'd painstakingly assembled—combing through yard sales and talking some athletes into donating items that had gathered dust for years—to create the museum she maintained in the association's offices. I allowed myself to daydream about what it would be like to have a race so impressive that Gloria would call and ask for my shoes. She personified the connection between the marathon and the city. Her passion for that long, paved ribbon of collective memory was contagious, and I caught it.

Race day cemented my new love affair with the distance and the one-of-a-kind setting. A powerful, icy nor'easter blew up; the forecast was so dire that the BAA considered canceling for the first time in the marathon's century-plus history. In the end, temperatures warmed enough to turn snow into sheets of rain and the wind subsided, making conditions merely miserable rather than intolerable. My goal-time debate with the brothers proved to be moot—everyone, including me, was forced to run with more restraint, and I finished in 2:44. Fans braved the weather to line the course. I recognized the landmarks Dick Beardsley had described. I was retracing the path of icons. I loved every cold, soggy, challenging step.

A year later, I returned to Boston for the US women's Olympic marathon team trials with more anticipation than I'd brought to any other event. I nurtured big ambitions of a top-three finish that would earn me a slot for the 2008 Beijing Games, but ambition didn't translate to expertise or the learned science of fueling properly before and during the race. Running fourth at Mile 21, just eight seconds behind the runner I needed to pass to earn the third Olympic spot, my glycogen stores hit empty, and I finished thirteenth on dead legs. The fail felt massive and avoidable, but I simply didn't have enough experience. Natalie's words were among the few that got through to me that day. "If I'm investing my money in someone right now, it's you," she said. "You're going in the right direction. You're going up." It was a good reminder that this had been my first taste of the unique intensity of the trials.

For every moment of triumph, for every instance of beauty, many souls must be trampled.

Hunter S. Thompson, author's note,
The Proud Highway

———

MEANWHILE, THE HANSONS had their first Olympian: Brian Sell, who had finished third at the men's trials in New York City the previous fall. Kevin formulated a plan to have him better equipped than anyone else for the sweltering heat and humidity of the Beijing Games. Brian put his head down and put in the literal sweat equity, bundling up in the middle of the sticky Michigan summer for his daily runs and finishing off the last and most important few weeks of the segment in Orlando working out in the middle of the day. It was a well-meaning effort by both the athlete and the coach, but after Brian finished twenty-second in 2:16, well off his personal best, it was clear he'd been overcooked. I felt a ton of empathy for him. He'd put so much in his life on hold to make that team—too much to have his expectations fall so short of reality. This wasn't a major like Boston, where he could come back and refine his training the following year. He'd wagered double or nothing and lost.

Brian would wind up leaving the Hansons at the end of the following year. It wasn't just about Beijing—he'd been unhappy and resentful for a while with the way the group was structured, and he was vocal about it. Watching the tension play out was like watching Natalie go first, testing our parents. Brian made it clear to me that he saw an imbalance in who was doing the work and who was taking the credit. Did the Hansons make him, or did he make the

Hansons? The brothers expected more gratitude, and it appeared to me that they resisted the idea of gratitude going both ways. I thought both coaches and athletes deserved thanks when things were going well, but I could see how the Hansons' dual role as business managers made things more complicated.

The longer I stayed in Michigan, the higher the odds were that it would become a more permanent home, and I still wasn't ready to make that commitment. I had become curious enough to explore my options and had my own flirtation with leaving. Amy Hastings, who had moved to the Mammoth Track Club in California, seemed genuinely happy training with Terrence Mahon, and the idea of getting the band back together had a certain appeal. I reached out to Terrence before the 2008 Chicago Marathon that fall; after I finished fifth, the top American in a personal best 2:31, he let me know he'd be happy to have me.

I took a hard look at what I'd be getting into. Amy had been a step or two better than me when we were at ASU, and I still vividly remembered running myself into the ground trying to keep up with her. Looking back, I could see why I'd felt dead on so many race days. Our fitness levels were more even now, but I still wondered about slipping back into that dynamic just when I was coming into my own. I tried to be pragmatic and separate the beneficial aspects of the Hansons' coaching from the doubts I was starting to have about their business approach. Could I keep one and not the other? The Hansons still had a lot to offer me, I was an increasingly valuable asset to their program as I progressed, and my intuition told me that our partnership had many more miles to go. Loyalty and obligation won out. I bought into the idea that I should dance with the ones who had brought me, and tabled the idea of a coaching switch—indefinitely.

◆ ◆ ◆

I LOOKED AT every result as a chance to assess whether I should continue running. That self-imposed pressure pushed me to a personal best 2:27:53 and tenth place at the 2009 World Championships. Breaking 2:30 was a big deal at the time, and I had smashed it. It was also the first time I'd competed against Kara Goucher, someone I'd admired since my college days. I was able to close the gap on her in the last mile, and finishing just 5 seconds behind her told me how far I had come.

Ryan and I and another Team USA marathoner, Zoila Gomez, celebrated by hopping around Europe for a couple of weeks. We purposely made Zurich a destination in hopes of seeing the IAAF Golden League meet there, but predictably, as the most prestigious circuit in professional track and field, it was sold out. We called every connection we could think of. No luck. So we settled for buying some cheap box wine and stood on the sidewalk outside the

Letzigrund stadium, pressed up against a gate that offered a partial view of the track, peering in.

Our efforts were rewarded. Dathan Ritzenhein put in a huge kick on the final lap to finish third in the 5,000-meter and set a new American record of 12:56.27—following in the footsteps of stars such as Steve Prefontaine, Marty Liquori, and Bob Kennedy, whose previous record had stood for thirteen years. Dathan was a fitting heir, one of the "big three" US men earmarked for stardom along with Alan Webb and Ryan Hall. They all graduated from high school in 2001, the same year as me, and generated massive hype every time they were at the same event. Dathan was from Michigan, and we had followed his progress closely. He'd already made one Olympic marathon team, he had just joined Salazar's training group earlier that year, and his future appeared to be limitless.

Chicago 2010 was my next big target. Nagging foot pain forced me to do some cross-training on the AlterG, an anti-gravity treadmill that can be set to a percentage of body weight to mitigate impact. Even with that subpar buildup, I lowered my personal best again with a 2:26:20. My first big paychecks went toward reinvesting in any little thing that could help me improve. I bought decent health insurance and moved out of the team ranch house into an immaculate home on a massive stretch of wooded property with a good friend and coworker from Moosejaw, Katie Altherr. A casual runner and avid skier, Katie was detached from the elite running scene, exactly the kind of roommate I wanted at the time.

Each success bought me time to keep doing what I was doing, but also raised the bar higher for what I needed to do next. I thought of it as a parallel kind of endurance—I had to survive to succeed, and succeed to survive long term. So, how could I push beyond what I'd done in Chicago? It was tempting to think about lopping another chunk of time off my personal best, and that pointed toward the London Marathon, with its similarly fast course and pacers who set the table for world record attempts. But there was more than one way to test my limits. I had reached the point where I needed to put myself in a true race scenario, without pacers out front doing the work, where I would have to make race moves and decisions on the fly. The uniquely tricky nature of the Boston course and the always unpredictable April weather there would put the onus on me not just to outrun my competition but also to outthink them. Calibrating and fine-tuning my target splits—pace per mile—and putting the right effort in on the appropriate sections of the course rather than blindly following what the race leaders did would set me up to run the final 10k better than any other woman.

Over breakfast in late 2010, Kevin, Keith, and I went over my spring options, weighing the pros and cons. London's prestige and forgiving terrain beckoned, but a big performance on American soil would always be more valuable than a fast time abroad.

"I think I can win in Boston," I said. "I've watched this race, and the winners aren't doing anything I can't do. It's possible."

I knew the outside world might find that audacious, but all I cared about was the people at the table, and I was confident they were on the same page. And we were a dangerous team when we were all on the same page.

◆ ◆ ◆

I'D NEVER TOPPED 100 miles a week before 2007; as I prepared for Boston 2011, shuttling back and forth between Michigan and Florida's friendlier climate, I was stringing together four or five 120-mile weeks in a row. Kevin's favored workouts for the last, crucial weeks of the marathon build were familiar to me by then: 16 miles at marathon pace of 5:29 per mile; 2 × 6 miles at 5 seconds faster than marathon pace, 5:24, with 10 minutes of rest; an 8-mile tempo workout, half at 5:29 and half at 5:24; and a long run of 20 miles. Recovery days meant 14 miles in the morning and 4 in the evening. With ten days to go, I tapered—to a 90-mile week. I approached every mile, every meal, every strength workout, and every minute in between (except Saint Patrick's Day, because I am human) with the mindset of a Boston Marathon champion. Every decision I made—doing second runs, drills, and strides outside in nasty winter conditions without a second thought, passing on beers after a long Moosejaw shift, lights out by ten o'clock for a minimum of eight hours of sleep—was based on a question and a challenge to myself: *Will this help me become a champion? Act as if you are the thing you are trying to become.* I loved feeling how consistent I was throughout the block and the narrow focus I had on my goal, things I had lacked before. I sensed my body adapting to the cumulative fatigue and getting stronger.

Those months gave me ample time to immerse myself in visualizing how the race would unfold. I would ignore any rash early moves; the first twenty miles were about getting to the real start line as fresh and efficiently as possible. By the three famous inclines known as the Newton hills, I would have worked myself into the lead pack, ready to race and be an aggressor from any point after the pack put Heartbreak Hill in the rearview. For the last 10k, I wanted to be in a position to dictate rather than react.

I pictured how it would feel to grind up the series of hills and how I would let my legs stretch out on the downhills, not recovering but using gravity to press the pace. I pictured the crowds growing and the roar swelling. I could smell the stale beer from the roadside parties and the exhaust of the lead vehicles in front of me. I could feel sweat trickling down my temples and stickiness on my palms from grabbing, drinking from, and discarding fluid bottles along the course. And I *always* pictured myself getting stronger each mile, laying waste to the competition, and turning onto Boylston Street alone—a bold vision, since the last few women's races had been decided by three seconds or less. I visualized celebrating in the final few strides and exactly how the tape would give way as I broke through.

Anyone witnessing the work I was doing knew I had a shot, but few were there to see it. Kara Goucher was attracting most of the advance media coverage with her story line of hoped-for redemption. She'd placed third in New York City in 2008 and again at Boston 2009—an excruciating finish where she was outsprinted by two East African runners on Boylston Street. Kara took a year off, had a baby son, and came back in good form at the NYC Half Marathon in March. I didn't pull punches in my own prerace interviews, saying that if I was with the leaders after twenty miles, I'd have a chance to win. I was fairly sure no one other than the people on my team believed me.

The stakes in Boston were higher than most people knew. Ryan and I had a bet: If I won, but he was faster, I would have to buy him a Corvette. We'd been training together for a few years by then, and our trajectories were crossing, on paper and on the road. When I caught him in the last mile of Chicago 2010, he started running alongside me. A lovely moment, yes, but it couldn't last. I didn't want people to think he was pacing me, and I was gunning for the top American time of the year—plus the Brooks bonus and the pride that would go with it. "I gotta go," I said, and pulled away. I beat Ryan by one second, bested Magdalena Lewy-Boulet by two seconds for fastest American of the year, and landed myself in fourth on the all-time US list.

This Boston block was special. Ryan and I were targeting the same race and a very nearly identical goal time. I was too fit for him to have much of a chance, though, and we both knew it. If he did buck the odds and run faster, I figured he would deserve the car, and I would deserve a driver.

◆ ◆ ◆

IT WAS FORTY-SIX degrees at the start, with a fourteen-mile-per-hour tailwind on much of the course—an ideal day for racing. As I had hoped, a group went out too hard, trying to cover a ferocious move by Kim Smith of New Zealand. Kara chased her for a bit, then dropped back and hung on with a slowly shrinking group of contenders. Emotion seemed to be driving the pace rather than common sense. They'd power ahead of me as the fans' decibel level rose in each little town, then slow down again, allowing me to close the gap somewhat, but I was by myself from 15k on. I felt completely composed, cranking out the splits I wanted, keeping my eyes on the bodies falling regularly off the chase group.

Smith still had a sizable lead through Wellesley, but near the Newton fire station, her calf seized up, and she stumbled. She was done, and would step off at 30k. Kara was another casualty of the pace. "Keep your eyes up," I said as I passed her in the Newton hills. I knew there were plenty of bodies about to go backward and I wanted to encourage her. But the grind in the hills, after the effort she'd already put in, was a little too much for her. She was dropped and ran most of the rest of the race alone.

I rejoined the lead group for good on Heartbreak Hill and churned up the incline with two Kenyans, Sharon Cherop and Caroline Kilel, and 2008 Boston champion Dire Tune of Ethiopia. Suddenly, after all that time on my own, I had company—and a soundtrack. The roar from both sides of the road had an underlying buzz of surprise: An American was in contention. I was completely focused on racing, but it was impossible to miss the chants of "U-S-A! U-S-A!"

I took the lead as we crested Heartbreak, exactly as I'd visualized.

Tune fell away.

Four miles to go.

Now I have to break them.

Except I couldn't. It was a drag race all the way into the city among Cherop and Kilel and me, down Beacon Street, through Coolidge Corner, onto the broad sweep of Commonwealth Avenue, past the Citgo sign with its distinctive red triangle, right up to the two most legendary turns in distance running.

Right on Hereford. Left on Boylston. All three of us made the last turn together, and then Kilel and I forged ahead and broke Cherop. Kilel surged into the lead. I responded, digging deeper than I thought possible, and retook it. The crowd packed behind the barriers was going bananas, delirious at seeing an American on the brink.

The weeks and months of learning how to run tired had funneled down to this: After twenty-six miles, I had to sprint for the win. It was the best- and worst-case scenario rolled into one. It was Beardsley-Salazar in 1982. It was Cheruiyot-Njenga in Chicago in 2006. It was me and one other runner, within sight of the tape and a life-altering outcome.

I didn't have time for reflection. I kicked, felt empty space next to me.

Right foot, left foot.

My right calf locked up. On the next foot strike, my left.

Fuuuuuuuccckkk.

Knots had formed instantly; in one beat, I went from full stride to hobbled. Helpless, I watched Kilel pass me for the final time and collapse past the finish line as I took the last few steps.

As she lay crumpled on the ground, weeping, I bent over

with my hands on my knees, trying to breathe through a level of depletion I'd never experienced before. I lifted my head and stared back up the course—a thousand-yard stare of disbelief. After months of daily, absolute conviction that I'd stand on the podium wearing the olive wreath, I had to put aside that vision and accept that I was not the Boston Marathon champion. History—and an end to twenty-six years of American futility—had eluded me by two seconds.

Hollowed out and numb, I went through the motions for the next few hours. The running world hailed my result—2:22:38, the fastest ever by an American woman at Boston—as a breakthrough success. Now that I knew what it took to get here, how ideal my build had been, how everything had to fall exactly the right way to get this shot, all I could think about was whether I'd ever have another one. It was hard to be gracious when people fawned over my "potential." I couldn't hear it as anything but a polite word for "You haven't done shit yet."

"It went perfect for me, minus not winning," I told reporters.

It took days for me to understand the impact of my performance and find validation in the pain. The ever-optimistic Ryan gave me a healthy, helpful dose of perspective, reminding me that this was far from my last finish line and encouraging me to celebrate how far I'd come. More perspective sank in when I walked back into Moosejaw for my regular shift four days later. My coworkers gave me a standing ovation, then steered me to all the orders that had piled up while I was away. Life hadn't stopped when my timing chip did.

I reminded myself that only twenty-four hours before, no one had taken my chances seriously. I'd done the right work to put myself in a position to win. My prerace statements had been justified. My confidence hadn't been outlandish. My career path made sense. I had become an expert at the distance and on this famous course; I understood what it meant to leave a hundred percent of my heart on these roads. It made me believe I could compete with anyone in the world in the marathon. I had leapfrogged into the top tier of the distance running scene, and in nine months, I'd be racing for an Olympic team spot at the US trials, aiming to fulfill a childhood goal and make a statement.

It was a mark of how deeply Boston had gotten into my blood that two hours into the race, in the Newton hills, I'd put my hand to my ear and then gestured to the crowd in the universal sign for "Louder"—and they had obliged. It was completely out of character for me, but I was someone else between the curbs that day. It was okay to want to crush competitors' souls, and totally fine to be flashy and want all eyes on me, attitudes I detested away from racing. Something shifted in me when I heard the fans respond. They were invested in me, they hung on every step down the last straightaway, and I could feel them break along with me when the win slipped away. I had lived in San Diego and Tempe and suburban Detroit, but it turned out I'd found my home course in Boston, a city that had readily adopted me.

◆ ◆ ◆

JOSH COX AND I first met in person at a summer 2011 running expo in San Diego, where we'd both grown up—our first bond, and an important one. He'd gone to Christian High School in El Cajon, east of the city, and his fanaticism for the Padres exceeded even my family's. I knew of Josh from his precocious distance running accomplishments. Unlike me, he had embraced the marathon and even longer races at an early age. He was the youngest competitor in the 2000 US Olympic men's marathon trials, finishing in eighteenth place at age twenty-four, and had set the national 50k record in 2009, two years before we met. He had a strong handshake and a wide grin that entered the room before he did. I was inclined to like him right away.

I was appearing at a Dodge event brokered by the Hansons, with half my fee going to me and half to the brothers' Original Distance Project. It was the first business opportunity I'd been offered outside our team contract, and the fact that they had set the bar so far above the industry standard of fifteen percent took me by surprise. The Hansons had gotten me to this point, and I had rewarded them with a milestone for their program. On the other hand, I knew that my higher profile would put my relationship with the brothers under stress.

The terms that had felt fine to me when I turned pro didn't fit any more. I was increasingly edgy about feeling indebted and possibly one injury away from having no income. The structure that put the Hansons in the role of financial gatekeepers felt out of balance now, and it was no surprise that it reminded me of the dynamic with my father, when I couldn't separate running from the emotion embedded in that relationship: "Do x, y, and z, or I'll take this away from you and remind you how much I spent on it." Now that I was a professional, I owed it to myself to draw boundaries where they belonged and make sure my business plan was sound. I had taken mental notes on how Brooks had evolved under CEO Jim Weber's tight focus on performance shoes and determination to establish the company as tops in the market in that realm. I wanted the best in the business in each category on my team: coaching, physio, financial. That meant having someone to represent my interests above and beyond and help me sort through my unease with the business side of the ODP. Even the longest running careers were short compared with most jobs, and I needed to make sure mine would be personally and financially sustainable.

I reached out to Josh shortly after Boston for help in securing new sponsors and appearance opportunities. He had

represented himself throughout his running career, other
than a brief stint with a prominent Italian agent that ended
once Josh got a close look at the way he did business. Josh
still had half a foot in competitive running and was con-
templating getting into real estate when I contacted him. He
impressed me as a straight arrow, but he also shared my
growing distaste for the rigid conventions of the running
world and the way agents and athletes in our sport often
defaulted to them. He agreed with me that coaches had no
business writing athlete contracts. We both understood the
importance of fighting for the best deal, not just signing the
first deal. After studying the industry from the inside for a
few years, I fully believed something Josh repeated often:
"You don't get what you deserve, you get what you negotiate." I could tell that he would be invested in me in a way
the Hansons couldn't be.

It all added up to the realization that hiring Josh to be
my agent would be another way of investing in myself—
spending money wisely to make professional headway. My
Hansons-Brooks contract didn't expire until the end of the
year, but I asked Josh to represent me for any other en-
dorsement deals or appearances. I liked the idea of being
his first client, with a hands-on role in my own future. We
would give each other the tools to set us both up for success. It felt like the right kind of mutual obligation.

When I was ready to make the change, I told the Hansons I was bringing Josh on. It's easy to say "Nothing

personal—just business," but a little harder to execute. I hoped the brothers would see the mutual benefit in a different blueprint and a chance to free them up to do what they did best. They seemed relieved at having my individual business opportunities taken off their plate, but I sensed some tension. I chalked that up to Josh's skill at marketing himself and, at times, attracting more attention than other runners in his cohort—including my ODP teammates.

Over the next few months, Josh and I collaborated to build brand partnerships that matched my goals. I found the process liberating. It created a strong foundation of trust between us and opened up my road in more ways than one. In talks with a new sponsor, Josh negotiated a $5,000 bonus for any race win, for up to four races per year. As the days on the calendar dwindled, I hunted down openings for cheap wins at fun runs. I won a Turkey Trot, a Jingle Jog, and a New Year's Resolution Run with little competition and high returns. We called these outings "Filthy Rich Saturdays" and planned to blow the money on something outrageous.

Being on the road, smiling through appearances, and refueling our social energy over beers afterward reinforced how well we got along personally. We could chat nonstop but also appreciated quieter moments and knew intuitively when to let a conversation breathe. We agreed on principles ninety-nine percent of the time, and the few times we didn't, he'd wait until we'd both cooled off and then lay out how he might approach things differently. Josh told me he would do every deal of mine as if it were his own, and underlined his point by telling me a story about Maurice Sendak, the famous author and illustrator of *Where the Wild Things Are* and other children's books. Sendak often responded personally to fan mail from kids with notes and drawings. One mom wrote him back and said her son was so excited to get a card from his hero—complete with a drawing of a Wild Thing—that he stuffed the whole note into his mouth. The image made both of us laugh. My contracts, Josh said, should be just as appetizing.

His first major negotiation for me was my next appearance fee for Boston. I was confident I would make the London 2012 US Olympic team at the trials that January, which meant no spring marathon, so we set our sights on ensuring that I would get what I was worth the following year. The back-and-forth on that deal brought me an unexpected bonus: a warm friendship with the person on the other side of the table, Mary Kate Shea.

MK had been with John Hancock since 1999, but this was the first time she'd been in charge of recruiting and handpicking the elite field. I had taken an instant liking to her when I'd met her the year before; we could converse easily about all things running but connected mostly over books, travel, good coffee, and good dogs while throwing back drinks in the evening. The process of talking through the 2013 athlete contract highlighted her strengths as a businesswoman and a human. I could press for what I wanted but still have a good laugh with her; I could pick her brain on serious topics and get honest feedback rather than the pandering and gamesmanship I felt from many people in the industry. MK cared about both the race and the people who ran it, and she was strong and ethical enough to balance the business and the personal. Her dealings with us were tough but infused with respect. I began to consider her an unofficial adviser of sorts, a mentor and role model.

Josh texted me when he sent over MK's offer: "You're going to want to eat this paper." My appearance fee now had an additional digit on it—a tangible sign of my value, of progress in my chosen profession, of how much my stock had risen. My little start-up had some legs.

MILE SIX

TRUE TO JOHN Ball's prediction, we slog through the first few miles, practically shuffling, in one big, amorphous pack. Nobody is interested in leading the way into the rain, the headwind, the cold. The nor'easter in 2007 was no joke, and 2015 was blustery, but nothing in my experience compares with this.

The first six miles are predominantly downhill. The race isn't won on those descents, but it can be lost there. Each runner's bottles, pre-filled with fluids to replenish electrolytes, carbs, and caffeine, are set up on tables at 5k intervals, and it's vital to hit them early and often. I found that out the hard way in 2008, when I didn't take in enough fluids and faded badly in the last five miles. On days like this, strategic hydration and nutrition fuel the metabolic systems that keep the body warm. If I let that slide, the energy I would expend by shivering would make me burn through my glycogen stores at a significantly faster rate than usual. Once I got in trouble, it would be impossible to scramble back, and I would find my fuel tank empty well before the finish line.

The fluid tables reserved for elite athletes have numbered spots for our bottles. Typically, I'm meticulous about my marathon nutrition plan and bottle preparation: silver for the first four stops, where it's an electrolyte-carb mix; yellow for two in the middle that have a shot of caffeine; back to silver; and a regular mix toward the end. In the stress and uncertainty of the last forty-eight hours, I'd slapped together my bottles without labeling them properly for the race organization. When I come up on the first hydration spot on the left side of the course, plans begin crumbling. The lead pack is huge, and chaotic, and practically jogging in the deluge. I have to weave through a crowd to get to the table without breaking my rhythm, such as it is. And then I see a bottle that's yellow, not silver, in my designated spot. It must not be mine. I leave it. A missed bottle isn't ideal, but I can't let it shake me up too much.

I'm very conscious of my new racing flats. They have more cushion than anything I've raced in before, and the thicker midsole makes my foot strikes feel a little less stable. They also feel loose and sloppy on my feet, but it's hard to separate whether that's about the actual fit or the fact that they're waterlogged and it's freezing, so I've lost all feeling in my feet. Then my heel gets clipped hard in the tight pack, and I stumble badly. If there were ever a good reason to drop out, it's taking a digger in the pouring rain and losing a crap ton of ground on the pack. Who could fault me after that? Yet I feel myself fighting hard to stay on two feet. I don't want that kind of excuse, and despite my calculated race plan, I know intrinsically that I'd rather finish if I can.

Aselefech Mergia of Ethiopia goes to the front and pushes the pace as we approach the Mile 6 mark, hitting it in a more respectable 5:35.9. If that continues, it projects to a 2:26:17 finish time—a top-ten time under normal conditions, but too rich for me or probably anyone else today.

Mile 1: 6:35.2
Mile 2: 5:55.1
Mile 3: 6:07.6
Mile 4: 5:52.6
Mile 5: 5:47.4
Mile 6: 5:35.9

Apparently I'm not alone in that thinking, because the pack slows collectively, and soon we're well up over six-minute splits again.

I search the sea of soggy, bobbing heads and make my way over to Shalane, who's churning along in a black-and-white jacket with a headband holding her hat in place. Her face underneath the visor looks stoic, as I would expect. She's a warrior, and it's early days in the race.

"Hey, it's not gonna be my day; I think I'm going to drop out soon," I said. "Let me know if you need anything."

Shalane grabs my shoulder. I can see genuine concern on her face. "Are you okay? Are you hurt?"

"Yeah. I'm just not feeling very good. If there's anything I can do to help you, let me know."

I hadn't premeditated what I was going to say, but I meant it. If I couldn't finish, why not be unselfish and take the brunt of the headwind off someone else? Shalane winning Boston back-to-back with New York would be a hell of a story, great for American running and clean athletes in general, and uplifting for the veterans who had stuck around. Like me, theoretically.

At the 10k mark, the pack is still very much intact. Nobody will be shaken by this pace this early in the marathon. We're merely running for transportation. The racing will happen miles down the road.

I come up on the second fluid table. As I strive to find logic in the chaos, I've now convinced myself that all my yellow bottles will be first, so I'm rattled yet again when I see silver. I hesitate for a second—*Is this mine?*—and then it's too late. I've passed up another chance to fuel. I berate myself for my sloppiness and hope this won't catch up with me later. I didn't think it would matter last night, since I wasn't even sure I would finish, but now at least a small part of me thinks I might go the full distance. If I want to keep that option open, I can't afford to miss another bottle, so I resolve to take the next one in my numbered spot, no matter what color it is.

We roll on into the storm. The conditions ebb and flow. It's consistently miserable, with rain so dense I can hardly see in front of me. Every so often, the weather ratchets up to a new degree of unbearable, with unrelenting blasts of frigid wind that stall my steps and slice through every fully saturated layer I'm wearing. Everyone is at risk of icing up. I knew I could tolerate a lot of discomfort, but these moments raise my personal pain threshold.

We've traversed the towns of Ashland, Framingham, and Natick, and we're approaching Wellesley, where college students usually line both sides of the course and create a tunnel of sound. Each familiar landmark is a tiny achievement, one step closer to where I might force myself to step off, just before the Newton hills.

If I did walk away, it would mark only the second time in my career that I'd failed to complete a race, a stat that would be recorded as DNF, or Did Not Finish. The first was after just two miles at the 2012 Summer Olympic Games in London. That was difficult enough; this feels even more drastic because it could be my final exit. I'm not convinced I'll ever run a major marathon again.

I shake off the doomsday scenario. At least the pace seems manageable now.

Mile 7: 5:49.6
Mile 8: 6:10.9
Mile 9: 6:23.8
Mile 10: 6:18.7
Mile 11: 6:22.2
Mile 12: 6:11.5

Somewhere between Miles 12 and 13, I feel someone nudge my shoulder. It's Shalane.

She says, "Hey . . ."

DREAMS AND DUST

WHAT IS THE shape, the sound, the texture of a dream realized? I found out when I took the last left-hand turn into the finishing stretch of the 2012 US Olympic marathon trials in downtown Houston on a cool, bright January morning. "Here she comes!" the public address announcer yelled, referring to Shalane, who was up ahead and about to break the tape, but it applied to me, too. This event was unlike any other—one day, one race, top three go to the Olympics, everyone else goes home—and I was about to finish second, eleven seconds ahead of Kara. As I ran that flat city block awash with cheers, past a ramrod-straight line of uniformed military personnel and red-white-and-blue placards emblazoned with the flags of Texas and the United States, I tried my best to soak in what this meant. I remembered to pull off my sunglasses so my face wasn't obscured. I was very ready for this close-up.

It felt both surreal and natural, considering how long I had visualized this moment and convinced myself it would happen. This result was the shining payoff for years of hard work. It validated the life path I had chosen, justified the Hansons' faith in me over the last six years, and instantly increased my marketing value. I was overflowing with hope and excitement at the prospect of racing on the biggest stage and stoked to celebrate with the people who had helped get me there: Ryan, the Hansons, the Brooks crew, Frank Browne, my sister, and my parents.

Seeing Amy come in fourth little more than a minute later, her eyes welling with tears, was a polar-opposite experience and brought on my only mixed feelings of the day. She was the one I would have loved to have standing beside me with a flag draped around our shoulders, ready to show what we could do with the whole world watching in a few months' time—the kind of moment we'd talked about on those long runs at South Mountain. Back then, I thought she had the better shot at becoming an Olympian. Now I had played a direct part in denying her a spot. Amy was green at the distance, and I knew her so well—too well. On the ropes late in the race, she went to the front of our four-woman leaders' pack in an attempt to dictate the pace one last time. It was a telltale sign she was in trouble and would crack if we kept doing what we were doing. There was no ambivalence on my part. I knew what she would expect me to do.

I broke away from the group celebration at the finish to give her a hug. One of our shared goals was still intact: I had no doubt we'd get to walk into the opening ceremonies in London together. The moment Amy missed the marathon team, she became an immediate favorite to qualify for the 10,000-meter event. I told her to get herself ready. I also knew there was nothing I could say that would make the moment less heartbreaking.

Shalane and Kara embraced me at the finish, but I was very conscious of being the outsider in that trio. The two of them were training partners, highly touted Nike athletes, world championship medalists, and experienced Olympians on the track. A brigade of Nike folks descended on the finish area, handing out gear, and Joan Benoit Samuelson arrived to congratulate the company's two It Girls. Coaches, agents, and family members hovered. The Hansons were out dealing with the rest of our team. Josh was running what would be one of his last elite races. I had told everyone else I'd see them in a few hours. My entourage consisted of Ryan, which was the way I wanted it.

Yet Shalane, Kara, and I were bonded in another sense: a cohort with common purpose, carrying high hopes and expectations. We brought both promise and experience to the table, continuing a steady progression from the 2000 Sydney Games, when only one American woman made the marathon qualifying standard. Deena Kastor's bronze medal in 2004 had been a huge inspiration, but no one was immune from the pitfalls and variables of our event; four years later in Beijing, she limped off the course at the 5k mark with a broken foot. Our results in majors proved we could run with the best, and putting multiple contenders on the start line showed real headway. The fact that I had made it this far with a less conventional approach reinforced the idea that there was more than one route to the top—a sign of depth I was convinced would benefit the sport.

Shalane was firmly established as the alpha runner of our generation, an athlete who'd been painted to me as a goddess so glowingly and consistently over the years that I felt simultaneously annoyed and intimidated by her before we ever met. She had my full respect, but I felt I had a long way to go to be able to earn hers. There was a fair amount of chatter in 2011 when Kara left Alberto Salazar's Nike Oregon Project to join her and coach Jerry Schumacher at the Bowerman Track Club in Portland, Oregon. I had no problem with Kara personally—she'd been pleasant enough when we were teammates at the 2009 World Championships, and we'd exchanged some collegial words at Boston 2011 when she ran a personal best and finished fifth. But the NOP was widely viewed in the running world—including by me—as a place where medical-ethical boundaries were obscured, at best. Kara's migration to Bowerman enabled her to stay in the Nike sphere, train with someone who would push her, and get out from under the cloud of distrust that trailed Alberto. I viewed it as a pure business decision.

I was seeing a lot of things through a business filter now, and it was giving me clarity. I wanted the Hansons to keep coaching me, but without the framework where they also served as agents, bosses, and landlords, and where we had to compete for the same finite meal budget from Brooks. My job was to give myself a career, not to be a cog in their system. I understood that they needed to look after themselves and their team first. Coaches helped make athletes, but athletes also helped make coaches, and it seemed more productive to find a way to work together without being distracted by underlying tension about who was the most important person in the room. I needed to feel more independent and self-determining after investing eight years of my life.

So, I gambled on myself. My Hansons-Brooks deal had lapsed on New Year's Day 2012, but I'd deliberately delayed starting contract talks with the Hansons until after the trials. Earning my spot on the Olympic team immediately increased my value and made good on that bet. For most of the relatively short history of the Olympic women's marathon, one runner had embodied the best hope for US success at each Games, and that story dominated the media exposure that led to financial opportunity. Joan had paved the way with her win in 1984, and Deena had deservedly inherited the mantle. Suddenly, our generation had a rotating cast of top women, any of whom could steal the show on a given day. Three individuals with strong backstories would translate to significantly more coverage, or "earned media"—the insider phrase for space you can't buy—priceless both for our respective sponsors and women's marathoning as a whole. In past Olympic years, we would have been competing for the biggest piece of the pie. The way I viewed it, we had a unique opportunity to make more pie.

This was the right time for me to step up and push for change within the Original Distance Project. The Hansons had just produced a second Olympian from their underdog group, and I figured they had more leverage now, too. I asked them to go to bat for me and the entire team, to ditch the single-year, bonus-only structure, and secure salaries and multiyear contracts from Brooks. This diverged from the way they'd always run the group, and I wasn't surprised when it created tension with Kevin. He often fixated on gratitude, and when I pushed for changes, he seemed to interpret it as a lack of appreciation. I got a forwarded email—forwarded accidentally, I think, although I'll never know—from him to Brooks, apologizing for being a pain in the ass because he was negotiating on my behalf. He was apparently limited in how much he was willing to advocate for me.

Josh had already done some of my secondary sponsorship deals. Now I asked him to take on my shoe sponsorship and race appearances as well. He found it difficult to untangle my contract from the training group's deal and wound up playing an integral part in the wholesale restructuring of the Hansons' new deal with Brooks. Finalized in June, the contract made performance-based stipends available in addition to bonuses, which immediately helped recruit better talent. In my case, Josh added an additional level of incentive payments once I became an Olympian—a status that wouldn't become official until I started the race in London—along with medal bonuses. I felt vindicated for having fought to set myself up for professional success and forging a cogent career path, and more comfortable having the coaching and business aspects separated. The Hansons seemed to accept the shift, yet in my mind, the relationship seemed strained. I sometimes wondered if the conflict was real or something I'd constructed—a means of proving one more person wrong.

◆ ◆ ◆

IT'S HARD TO imagine anyone more meticulous than Kevin when it came to breaking down a course. He had Boston down to a science, returning for training tours every year, tweaking and correcting our training to make sure we were ready for each section. This time Kevin was convinced that the unusual, twisting course design in London would be the difference maker. He wanted to prepare my body for the multiple turns and rhythm-breaking layout I would face on race day, when I'd have to turn hard while running hard. He laid out a London replica course with undulating terrain: some gentle, sweeping curves and numerous sharp ones.

I was usually open to Kevin's ideas, but I balked at this one and the crucial time when it was inserted in my training block. I couldn't manage the turns or find a rhythm or pace that would get me in top shape or, more important, provide any assurance that I was in shape. After my first couple of workouts on this course in early July, when I hadn't nailed a single split I wanted, I blew up: What the actual fuck? When he retold the story, Kevin said his daughter learned new swear words that day, and I don't doubt it. He heard and respected my frustration, and said he'd work on making a modified edition of the route. That became moot when I stepped out of bed the next morning and had a hard time putting weight on my right leg. I struggled through a seven-mile run that day. It would be my last on solid ground for some time.

I don't blame Kevin's mini-Olympic course for what happened next. I'd been out of sync that whole spring, with an unusual tightness in my stride. In hindsight, the injury had been creeping up on me for months. It was an irritant that felt like a deep itch for a few minutes at a time on a given run but didn't cause enough pain to make me consider backing off. Now, abruptly, it was something I couldn't ignore: a sharp, stabbing sensation in my groin, above my right leg. I wasn't one to panic—that never solved anything —so I defaulted to constructive denial. *I'll take a little time off. That fixes everything. Right? Two days, three days.*

Everything was presenting in my high hip, where it met the groin. I went to physical therapy religiously. A magnetic resonance imaging (MRI) scan showed nothing. Everyone concluded that the problem likely stemmed from inflammation, possibly hip flexor tendinitis. A cortisone shot didn't help. The only thing that gave me any relief was to place my hand deep in my groin, find the tender spot, and apply pressure. While frowned upon in social settings, the vaguely obscene gesture seemed fitting, given my rising sense that I was fucked.

I spent the next three weeks on the AlterG. It is a revolutionary device in the endurance sports world, but it was an instrument of torture in my situation. I was indoors, in front of a TV with *Toddlers & Tiaras* on a constant loop and the remote control perpetually out of reach, running in a plastic bubble, suspended by neoprene shorts for ninety minutes at a time, feeling claustrophobic and increasingly pessimistic. The movement was unnatural. I imagined it would be the closest I'd get to walking on the moon: part bound, part bounce. I didn't know whether my feet were landing under me evenly or if I was compensating with my stride. I tried to bury myself in routine—drive over, set up, run, shower, go home, and wallow—but my mind chased its tail in furious circles. *I have such a short time frame, this isn't really doing it, I'm just literally going through the motions right now.* Still, I showed up each day, sticking to my ingrained habit of putting the previous one behind me. Short-term memory is the athlete's friend. I kept clinging to the faint belief that maybe *today* things would miraculously turn a corner.

◆ ◆ ◆

I FLEW TO London unconvinced I would be able to finish the marathon. The question was whether I should even start. Kevin gave an interview to *Runner's World* magazine, breaking the news that I was struggling with an injury, and said he was "less and less confident" of my ability to race pain free. He said I would defer my decision on whether to run until I tested myself on "hard surfaces" once I got there. That was true. I was still allowing myself a sliver of hope.

I chose to allow myself something else as well: the chance to march in the opening ceremony with the US team. It meant several hours on my feet, but since I didn't think fresh legs would make any difference at that point, I didn't see it as a problem. Still, I wrestled with guilt about enjoying any aspect of the Games—until I got a message from Magdalena Lewy-Boulet, a former UC-Berkeley star whom I had admired since we met on my recruiting trip there more than ten years before. Magda, originally from Poland, had become a US citizen on 9/11. It meant the world to her when she made the 2008 marathon team and earned a chance to represent her adopted country, but a knee injury forced her to step off after 20k. She urged me to wring everything I could from the experience. "I made a huge mistake four years ago and opted not to go to the opening ceremonies," she wrote. "I got hurt while in Beijing and then DNFed and was too upset to go to the closing ceremony. Don't do what I did. You are an Olympian and always will be." I had brushed off similar well-meaning advice from others, but Magda knew what she was talking about. I took her words to heart. *I'm here. I chose to do this. Appreciate it. Otherwise just go home.*

That was how I found myself walking into the crazy kaleidoscope of noise, color, and light in London's Olympic Stadium with Amy, who had qualified in the 10,000, as expected. It was magnificent. Entering the spectacle in the middle of the show was disorienting, and I had very little idea of what was going on around us, but I knew we were in the center of something brilliant. It was strange and unique and rewarding, a moment that actually lived up to anticipation that had been building since I'd watched it on TV as a kid. We milled around the infield for a couple of hours, trying to piece together what was happening—too many moving parts to take in at once. I was fascinated watching the best athletes in the world geek out over the other best athletes in the world. And I was one of them, on the inside at last. The night was also a mental balancing act, as moments of pure awe and happiness alternated with self-scolding about how I wasn't entitled to feel that way.

A few days after the opening ceremony, Kevin, Keith, and I agreed that I should formally withdraw. My hip wasn't getting better, and I was resigned to what would happen if I tried to test it. I sent the official email three days before the race, triggering a total shit show. Rose Monday, the team leader for USA Track & Field, met me in the Olympic Village and escorted me down to the basement medical facility, saying the team doctor needed to assess me to determine whether anything could be done to help me start. When I emerged after an hour of treatment, my phone exploded with texts and voice mails. Kevin, who was traveling that day, had written a piece for the *Detroit Free Press* saying I was going to withdraw from the race. While he was in the air, Keith had discovered through official channels that if I scratched, I would have to pack up, vacate my room in the Village, and leave behind any US Olympic team gear, because if I didn't set foot on the course, I wasn't technically an Olympian. And USATF was prepared to fly Clara Grandt, the seventh-place finisher at trials, to London to take my place.

Two things sharpened my resolve over the next hour. First, because of the way my new contract had been written, the next four years of my life were predicated on having the title of "Olympian." Second, there really wasn't a viable alternate to step in for me. If Amy hadn't made the 10,000-meter team, it would have been a very different scenario. But she was my roommate in the Village, and I knew firsthand that she was fully committed to the track. So was Janet Bawcom, who had been fifth at trials. Deena, who'd finished sixth, was injured. We had heard through the grapevine that Clara was also hurt and had pulled out of her last start. No one else was credibly trained for the Olympic marathon at that point. I had finished top three at trials. Shouldn't I just start and see what happened? Keith and I agreed that I would tell USATF I still planned on starting. I tweeted, "My race, my call," to remind everyone it was my choice.

It was an endless couple of days waiting for the inevitable, but I felt a lot of support, some of it unexpected. Kara and Shalane both reached out, encouraging me to stand by my decision and not worry about the reaction—empathy I appreciated. Keith stepped up, talking through my concerns about the race, the injury, and the future over coffee every day. Thankfully, my good friend and ASU teammate Cody Sohn was in London and did a lot of listening as well.

My closest brush with greatness was achieved vicariously, through my official podium jacket. Like everyone else on the US team, I'd been issued the special Team USA uniform that medalists would wear on the podium. Once in

London, we discovered that everyone's gear sizes were mixed up. Sanya Richards-Ross, who had collected two previous relay gold medals in Athens and Beijing, had been given an XXL jacket. "You need one that fits more than I do," I told her, and handed over my ill-fitting size medium. It was a well-educated guess. Sanya won her first individual gold in the 400 the same day as the marathon. Her jacket looked fucking amazing.

◆ ◆ ◆

I'D BE LYING if I said I wasn't asking the universe for a last-second reprieve that would at least enable me to perform respectably. And truth is, I wanted to step on that course. Showing up, working hard, doing the right thing—all of what I'd done to get there made me feel I owed myself a shot, even if it was the longest of shots. But every athlete at this level works hard. If we all got what we deserved, the podium would be a crowded place.

I packed a bunch of ibuprofen, thinking I'd slug down four or five and see how far that got me. *Who knows? Leave the possibility open. Maybe I can cover the distance. That would be a win today.* Magda's message was still resonating. It was all valuable learning for next time, an idea that was fast gaining traction in my mind. The colder, rational part of me knew the drill. Stepping off the course at the start-finish after the first 2.2-mile loop, near the recovery and medical tents, was the efficient, practical, wise thing to do. I also packed my insurance card in case something really went south on the road.

Fittingly for my mood, it was pouring rain at the start on London's majestic, flag-lined Mall. My memory of the next fifteen minutes is blurry, other than the piercing pain I felt, like clockwork, on the first right-hand turn. There would be no miracles that day; in fact, I felt as if every extra step might lengthen my recovery. Kevin had arranged for Natalie and my parents to be standing in the crowd on the first mile, so they got a chance to cheer as they saw me go by, and I spotted a few friends in the throngs by the side of the road. When I reached the point where I knew I had to stop, barricades blocked egress from the course. I spotted Glenn Latimer, whom I knew from the London and Chicago Marathon organizations. "Hey. I'm dropping out," I said. He moved one of the barricades, leaving just enough space for me to slip through. "Come this way," he said. And that was the end of my Olympic experience.

I went back to the tents and changed my shoes. Someone told me there were reporters waiting for me in the interview area. I felt mildly surprised that anyone wanted to talk to me. Yet even in my numbness and dejection, I felt strongly about going out to face them. *It's a job. You can't just emerge on the good days and talk about how awesome you are. One more learning moment. Stay logical, stay composed, answer questions for five minutes. Then you can go off and be emotional.*

"The last month especially, I put everything I had into getting here," I said. "I think I have another Olympics in me, and it's valuable to know what the Village is like and what the starting room is like. Everything's been really bittersweet."

I was deluged with messages, mostly positive, but it was hard not to dwell on the scathing ones that called me selfish and deceptive for not giving up my spot. I expected restrained disappointment from my family and friends, but they were just happy I had achieved my childhood dream, and they were having a great time in London. My head swam: *You don't fucking get it. You don't understand how miserable this is.* I reminded myself that they were the people closest to me, the ones whose opinions mattered far more than anonymous trolls. By their standards, I was a huge success. That was weirdly comforting.

After London, a friend sent me an excerpt of a speech that Joan Didion delivered back in the seventies. Didion was an author-hero of mine whose essay "On Self-Respect" had become a credo for me; I'd once named her as my pick for a fantasy running partner.

This passage resonated with me when little else did:

I'm not telling you to make the world better, because
I don't think that progress is necessarily part of the
package. I'm just telling you to live in it. Not just to
endure it, not just to suffer it, not just to pass through
it, but to live in it. To look at it. To try to get the picture.
To live recklessly. To take chances. To make your own
work and take pride in it. To seize the moment.

> *Joan Didion, 1975 commencement address*
> *at University of California, Riverside*

◆ ◆ ◆

IT WAS ANOTHER two or three weeks before I got an accurate diagnosis. I thought I'd rested enough, and I was
chafing to run again, but when I tried, the pain returned. I
finally drove myself to the St. Vincent Sports Performance
Center in Indianapolis, where USATF athletes could seek
care. As it turned out, all the imaging and guesswork had
been focused on the wrong place. Another MRI on my hip
just happened to catch the top of a mid-femur nondisplaced
cortical stress fracture. In plain English, I had a good-sized
crack in my thigh bone, the biggest one in my body. The
prescription was more of the same: Stay off it. Hearing the
seriousness of the injury brought a strange relief. It justified
my inability to push through the pain, and it was something
I understood how to fix.

When I went home to California for my grandmother's funeral, I told my parents I would be sidelined for a while. My dad's emotion around it surprised me, but then again, the occasion brought emotion to the surface, and his own days of hard physical labor in the construction business had taught him not to play games with injuries. He wanted me to know it was okay to walk away, that he wouldn't be upset, that I was allowed to quit.

"I don't want you to be beat up and broken down when you're older," he said. "I want you to be able to be healthy."

I knew why he was worried. In his mind, our shared stubbornness and the work ethic he had hammered into me had contributed to my injury. I needed him to know that those exact qualities were what made me great at what I did. I didn't always appreciate how he'd gone about teaching me, but I appreciated what he had taught me. And I understood now, in a way I hadn't as a kid, that there was no one guidebook for parenting. Sure, we could have handled our relationship differently, but we'd both done our best at the time, and we'd always started from a place of love. In the moment, I just tried to reassure him. "Dad, now I have the best doctors in the country," I said. "I'm in a good spot."

On many days, though, my outlook was far darker. I indulged myself by hanging out with friends and going on a few benders—notably, driving to Cleveland for a Monday-night show by the band Of Montreal, a road trip I could describe only as constructive self-medication. Live concerts had always been a great release for me, a place where no talking was necessary to share a common experience. I abandoned myself to the music that night, crowd-surfing in a hall where everyone had come to see this brilliant indie band out of Athens, Georgia, and tried to forget the bigger picture.

Let's pretend we don't exist
Let's pretend we're in Antarctica . . .

I had a four-year contract with Brooks, but all I could think about was where I found myself right that minute: in danger of falling behind the pack. The Hansons had recruited some great new talent, and I had angst about becoming irrelevant on my own team. I circled Boston 2013 as a meaningful goal—after finishing second, nothing could have been more motivating—but soon concluded that was unrealistic and asked to defer for a year. When the race sent out a brief statement saying that I had withdrawn, my calendar yawned empty for the first time in years.

That was when I got an email from John Ball. He'd also run for Walt Drenth at ASU and was still based near Tempe, in Chandler, Arizona. I didn't know him well, but I knew of his reputation. Nominally a chiropractor, John did far more than crack backs. He had parlayed his genius into a practice that specialized in endurance sports athletes, using physical therapy techniques and an uncanny comprehension of human kinetics to find the root cause of injuries, cleaning up soft tissue damage with a restorative touch and getting athletes moving with maximum mobility and fluidity. He had seen the news that I'd scratched from Boston. "Hey, you should really come down here," he wrote. "You can run that race. We can get you ready for it." The note enticed me to fly to Arizona for a consultation, and we examined my latest MRI together in his office.

"That's a bad fracture," he said. "I can't believe you were trying to run on that."

I told him I wouldn't have if I'd known it was more serious than tendinitis.

"Do you think everyone was just afraid to be the person who had to tell me I wasn't going to be able to run in the Olympics?"

"No way. That crack is near the femoral artery. Nobody would have let you run on that."

John retreated from his initial optimistic assessment and told me the road back to top form would be long. His blunt words actually boosted my confidence. It was clear he was looking at my career holistically, from both an athletic and business perspective. He was brutally honest about what he thought my body could handle in the near term and also took a broader view of what I needed to do to maximize my career earnings, longevity, and potential. I put myself in his hands, fully aware I'd have to lean into the patience that the marathon had taught me.

◆ ◆ ◆

I ATTENDED BOSTON 2013 as an invited guest. I'd come a long way in my recovery, but I was still nowhere near ideal fitness. Doing an interview on Boylston Street under a cloudless sky that morning made me yearn to be racing instead. "This is the greatest finish line in our sport," I said. "This is where everybody wants to be today." I handled a few other obligations, and then Ryan and I went for a ten-mile run. It went so well that I almost pushed it to twelve.

I was showering in our room at the Fairmont Copley Plaza hotel when Ryan called out, "Did you feel that crazy vibration?"

Moments later, down in the hotel lobby, we began to understand what had happened—although it took hours to grasp the full scope of the tragedy. Two bombs had exploded in the crowds packed along the finishing stretch, killing three and wounding and maiming many more. The devastating images we were seeing on television were two blocks from us, yet we felt as helpless as if they were coming from thousands of miles away. Our concern quickly turned to the people we knew who were running that day, including Frank Browne. We were relieved when he showed up at the hotel, having somehow talked his way in, and we let him use our room to clean up. It was hard not to feel guilty from the insulated safety of lockdown—and angry at the act of terrorism that had caused so much suffering at this event I loved.

What happened in Boston a year later was extraordinary. All thirty-six thousand runners who were there—from the elites, to the first-timers, to the people who had been trapped on the course and unable to finish—had a dual motivation: We all wanted to do our best *and* give the middle finger to anyone who thought they could intimidate us from coming together.

After my finish—a more than respectable 2:23:54 for ninth place—I rested in the elite athlete recovery area at the Fairmont and watched Meb Keflezighi solo to the first American win since 1983. Ten years after his Olympic silver medal, he was the guy who everyone had written off as past his prime. Meb had also been sidelined by injury in 2013. On the day of the bombings, he'd made up his mind to run again the next year and win for his country. I'd had an intuition about him, especially after I saw his prerace interview. He talked about what he'd visualized, down to the way the flag would feel on his shoulders and how he would hold it up to celebrate. It was goose-bump–inducing to see him come down the homestretch, carrying through on exactly what he had pictured for months and months.

As someone who knew what it was like to be counted out, it put a smile on my face. Meb was so genuine, his family's journey from the East African country of Eritrea was amazing, and he'd come of age in San Diego—there was hardly anyone in the running world whose triumph I would have enjoyed more. When his wife, Yordanos, embraced him at the finish line, I remembered talking to her through my heartache after coming so close in 2011. "I just know you're going to win this one day," she'd told me. "I have this feeling, this belief in you." Meb had kept getting back up, kept insisting he deserved to be in the conversation, kept creating chances. He'd made this moment for himself possible, yet he'd also made it about something bigger, writing the names of the people lost in the bombings on his bib. It was instructive and inspiring.

◆ ◆ ◆

THERE WAS NO getting around the fact that my own faith in my running ability had been rattled by my fractured leg and slow climb back. At times, I wasn't sure I would ever return to my former self. Yet my faith in the relationship that had grounded me since my early days in Michigan had never been stronger. Ryan knew when to give me space, when to read me the riot act, and when to reassure me. He gave me a sense of security sturdier than any four walls.

We already shared a house in the woods and two big, boisterous dogs: a golden retriever named Miles, and Atlas, a Chesapeake Bay retriever. Natalie and I spent our childhoods pleading for a puppy without success, so, naturally, I had made dogs a big part of my life. Ryan and I ran with them, lazed around with them, and enjoyed the companionship and sheer entertainment they provided. Miles and Atlas were clearly our alter egos. He had Miles when we met, and they mirrored each other's boundless energy and gregarious nature. Atlas was the epitome of determined and came by it honestly. His breeder told us a great story: She'd been so proud of Atlas's father for retrieving a particular Canadian goose that she'd had a taxidermist preserve and mount it. The first time they left the dog alone in the house with his trophy, he ripped it off the wall. *Mine.* I admired Atlas's intensity, but it had to be channeled, and his behavior needed some adjustment. We enrolled him in hunt school, and I learned to shoot and work with him, doing what he was born to do.

Now Ryan and I were about to solidify our partnership with wedding vows. I had to laugh at the memory of what my dad said when I told him I was going to Michigan to give this professional running thing a try. "Don't meet a boy, get married, and never come home," he instructed. Mission accomplished. Maybe he knew something I didn't.

Our wedding was in the small town of Petoskey, a few hours' drive from our house in Rochester, toward the northern tip of the mitten on the sandy shore of Lake Michigan. Ryan, born and raised in the state, had always loved it "up north," as Michiganders say. The beaches and vast body of water appealed to the Californian in me, and both Atlas and Miles were meant to be somewhere they could swim.

We were hatching plans to buy a second home in nearby Charlevoix.

On August 24, 2013, we woke up before the sun and paid our dues to the fitness gods. I ran a twenty-miler with Josh driving along and crewing with water bottles. Ryan jumped on his bike and knocked out a fifty-mile ride with his best man, our onetime roommate Ryan DeCook. With work done for the day, we were able to fully unwind for the ceremony and reception.

In a place that felt like home. Surrounded by loved ones. It was truly perfect.

◆ ◆ ◆

THE FOLLOWING MONTH, I put my legs and my confidence to the test and ran my first full marathon in nearly two years, on a fast, flat course in Berlin. I had turned down a big appearance fee offer from New York, choosing to race away from the glare of the US media and the prospect of close questioning about my comeback. I was yearning to feel as if I was on my A-game again while simultaneously tempering my expectations. My main goal was not to embarrass myself, but if I fell short of my own standards, I knew I couldn't let it define me—I had to view it in the context of a larger process. It was a huge relief when I beat my modest 2:30 target by under a minute. I was finally trending the right way and ready to take on the task of redeeming London by making the team for the 2016 Summer Olympics in Rio de Janeiro. It seemed achievable, but there would be many thousands of baby steps in between.

My progress had been excruciatingly slow. As I labored toward Berlin, I had to try to celebrate incremental gains. I was used to reeling off miles at a pace that only a small percentage of people in the world could sustain, and found it hard to be enthused about jogging five minutes more than I did the previous day. My passion, it seemed, was conditional. I wouldn't be celebrating world-class results anytime soon. Could I enjoy the simple act of putting one foot in front of the other? Appreciate working up a sweat? Be stoked to trim a few pounds and fit back into my skinny jeans? I knew I needed to find something intrinsic to love about running.

With the encouragement of my friend Wesley Korir, the great marathoner who had just been elected to Parliament in his native Kenya, I decided to spend a few weeks in that country's Great Rift Valley, a cradle of distance runners where champions are born and made. There were a lot of reasons to choose that destination—warm weather, my first-ever taste of altitude training, my perpetual wanderlust—but the most appealing idea was locking into a training mentality where there would be zero distractions. At the main US training hotspots—in Mammoth Lakes, California; Flagstaff, Arizona; and Boulder, Colorado—there were always bars and people I knew. This would be different, fun, fresh.

I made my first trip there in the winter of 2014 as part of my buildup for Boston. Once I walked under the big red arch at the entrance to the High Altitude Training Centre in the town of Iten, life boiled down to basics. Canadian marathoner Lanni Marchant and I shared a room furnished with twin beds, matching nightstands and chests of drawers, a toilet, a sink, and a shower that usually dispensed hot water. At six o'clock in the morning, I could join nearly three hundred local athletes of varying levels who met up to run the network of dirt roads that wend through surrounding villages, capillaries that connected to the main paved artery that led out of Iten. They were welcoming, and their body language showed how fully they were embracing the moment. Their numbers also helped me understand how superior their feeder system was to ours, how much deeper. On other days, I preferred to explore on my own or in a smaller group, or share some miles with Lanni, who had been running these roads the past few winters.

One thing remained constant: the clouds of brick-red dust that billowed up from our collective heels. That dust instantly became part of me, settling in my teeth and in my ears, caking on my skin, with rivulets of sweat running through it. It made me feel as if profound appreciation were permeating my soul. I found myself back in a headspace I hadn't inhabited since I was a kid, with a sense of peace and resolve and the answer to a question that had been tugging at me for a while. Yes, running was compatible with who I was—it was a continuing education, a ticket to see the world, delve into different cultures, and keep growing as a human.

I'll carry mental snapshots of that place forever. Runners of all types kicked up dirt on the roads of Iten: fellow elite athletes, tourists striving to rub shoulders with their heroes, and little kids, the next wave of world-beaters, running barefoot beside us *mzungu*—white people—for as long as they could, yelling "How are you? How are you? How are you?" Cattle farmers walked the roads with their herds, telling you not to worry because *their* cattle were polite. I arranged for one of the Kenyan men to run with me for a week and show me local routes for a few shillings—or about twenty dollars. It took just one memorable miscommunication for me to understand that the Kenyan mindset toward that work would be different. I requested an easy 20k loop from my pacer only to find myself way out in the countryside with my odometer at 30k and counting.

"Bro, where are we?"

"It's just seven more."

"No, no, no—I said 20k!"

"It's just a little over. You need to run, right?"

Various members of Kenya's running royalty had pieces of the action. Multiple road racing and cross-country world champion Lornah Kiplagat (no relation to Edna) founded the Iten training center. When you struck it rich in that world, you bought a hotel there, kind of like Monopoly. I saw other great athletes, including 2012 Boston winner Sharon Cherop, casually mixing with the masses. We connected for a run, a masala chai, and a viewing of her wedding video that showcased her beautiful cake shaped like the Boston Marathon trophy.

Being in Kenya also helped reaffirm the self-belief I'd had since 2011, when I sprinted down Boylston Street with Caroline Kilel. That had gone a long way toward breaking down any mystique that enveloped the East African contingent. I knew I had the strength and leg turnover to compete with them. Their desire was a different matter, and as much as I studied it and tried to tap into it, I realized it was next to impossible for an American athlete to comprehend how a Kenyan's life changes after winning a major. Instead, I reminded myself of what I was giving up—weeks away from Ryan, our home, our dogs—to sharpen my commitment. While I was still hungry for that one great win, my long, slow climb back to full fitness made me realize that consistently performing at a high level over a long career was just as much if not more of a challenge.

I also recognized there were some factors that were out of my hands. In the years after London 2012, investigations revealed inconsistent drug testing and rampant doping taking place in some regions. Russian doping scandals had already eroded faith in the worldwide anti-doping system; now East African dominance, long assumed to be a function of motivation and genetic talent, came under scrutiny. I was worried enough about perceptions that I asked around. Would the simple act of training in Kenya for a few weeks hurt me or raise any eyebrows? People mostly reassured me. "Well, you're with the Hansons. Everyone really trusts them." My Kenyan connections were Wesley and Lornah, whom everyone respects and admires. The fact that I had to think it through was a tough reality of my sport.

Kenyan dust is still part of me. Traveling, immersing myself in the unknown, being in a new environment, seeing that there's more than one way to do things, and steeping myself in a situation that's unusual and uncomfortable—I've relished those experiences for my entire running life. They speak to some need I have to externalize that *otherness* I've always felt. Travel generally reminds me that most people are good-hearted, ready to look out for a stranger. It takes leaving the comfort zone and going there to understand it.

◆ ◆ ◆

FOR FOUR YEARS, I thought of the 2016 Olympic marathon trials in Los Angeles as a giant flashing neon sign: the Second Chance Saloon. Getting back to the Summer Games would justify my decision to start in 2012, which continued to rent space in my head. It was a shit ton of pressure to put on myself. And, perversely, I loved it.

My mindset wasn't dissimilar from four years before: Top three go to the Games. It's not like you get a first-class seat if you win, or you have to carry everyone's bags if you're third. Temperatures were in the low seventies at the start and would rise to eighty degrees over the next two hours—good news for me and my desert-tested psyche, but my game plan going in was still conservative. I stayed tucked into the group, biding my time, letting attrition take care of itself and making sure I was in position to execute in the last 10k.

The other favorites had shuffled their alliances since 2012. Kara had returned to her college coaches, while Shalane and Amy had trained together at Bowerman. The two of them went off the front at Mile 10, pushing most of the top runners in the field to their limits way too early. I knew that those who covered the move would fade. I had studied and taught myself how to close out the last 10k of a marathon better than anyone, reeling off the splits that would ensure nobody could catch me over that section, and knowing that runners ahead of me would lose serious ground. It was just math and logic, a standardized test I knew how to pass.

The pace and the heat combined got to Shalane and she started to dehydrate, cramp, and wobble in the last few miles. Amy urged her on until Shalane ordered her to go ahead in the finishing stretch. I moved to the far side of the road when I passed her, wanting to avoid saying or doing anything distracting. Elation and relief surged through me as I rounded the last turn to the finish line, all alone in another perfect second place. After months of managing the weight of being a favorite to make the Olympic team, it was time for a deep exhale. I had gotten it right. Again. I turned around to see Shalane stagger across the line and collapse into Amy's arms, securing the third slot. Kara was the odd woman out this time, in fourth.

LA sealed our team's conviction that we were primed to do something special in Rio—a conviction that connected us and also made us hypercompetitive. The top American surely would have an excellent shot at an Olympic medal. I was thrilled for Amy, who was racing at a new level, and I sensed that Shalane had come to respect me and take me seriously as an athlete. I was going to have to run at another level, too. The training group mentality that had become part of my DNA at Hansons served me well, helping me think of us as one unit even though we weren't physically together in the weeks before we traveled to Brazil. We were all pushing one another with maturity and awareness that success breeds success, and together we were raising the game of marathoning in the United States.

I skipped the opening ceremony in Rio. This trip was about business. Or, more accurately, unfinished business. I wanted to achieve for myself, but zooming out, I also understood what that could mean for our generation and for the one coming behind us. I wanted to call myself an Olympian and feel like I wasn't a fraud. I remembered the sage words of Dr. Dave Martin, the US team physiologist, who liked to tell athletes to try to capture the electricity of the Games without getting electrocuted. I had stuck my fork in a socket in London, but I told myself that all the shocks I'd absorbed would be useful this time. I was in great shape, and my motivation, that outsider's attitude I used for fuel, had never been more intense.

◆ ◆ ◆

A FEW MINUTES after noon on Sunday, August 14, Shalane, Amy, and I sat in the postrace cooldown area behind the Sambadrome in Rio, trying to process what had just happened. Lively Brazilian music, fueled by thumping samba drums, pounded in the parade grounds built to host the city's famous Carnival, but we weren't in a partying mood. We had all placed in the top ten in the Olympic marathon on a sweltering day, the best collective finish for American women in history. I was proud of my effort but beyond perplexed at the outcome, and Shalane and Amy felt the same way. We had run so strongly. Why hadn't we been factors when the real racing began? Shalane had closed out the race better than I'd ever seen her, yet finished sixth in 2:25.26. I crossed the line 42 seconds later in seventh place. There was none of the usual pop or drive in my legs as I watched the leaders disappear; the top five all went under 2:25. Amy had battled stomach distress and hung on for ninth.

We openly shared our unease and disgust. *What was that?* Something did not add up. We all knew this race had been dirty, and speculated that medalists would be busted. I predicted two women in the top five would be banned from competition within a year. We'd been convinced we could pick up where Deena had left off and help inspire the next generation, yet rather than reaching the podium again and building momentum for the future, we might as well have been running in place. Our disappointment was profound.

It was a pivotal moment for Shalane and me. I had never really seen her let down her guard, but we were on the same page that day. As we walked out to face reporters, we knew that talking about doping would sound bitter and callous. Saying nothing felt like complicity, but we didn't think we had a choice. And we weren't wrong. The gold and silver medalists in Rio, Jemima Sumgong of Kenya and Bahrain's Eunice Kirwa, would later fail drug tests or have adverse biological passport findings and serve bans. Yet, in the ultimate insult to other athletes, not to mention sports fans, they got to keep their Olympic placements and medals.

In those moments after the finish, the drumbeat in my head was this: *so much work, so little payoff.* A sport that I thought was straightforward and objectively measured— fastest from point A to point B—was actually rife with politics and people gaming the system. What I had always viewed as the pinnacle of my sport had crumbled for me in two very different races four years apart. When I called Kevin to rehash the race, he sounded so disappointed he couldn't be bothered, so I hung up. I got the sense my inability to achieve a medal was considered a failure, and he was concerned that my "failure" reflected on him.

I didn't want to waste all the work I'd invested in my body and mindset, and I didn't want to give in to disillusionment. I'd put the Olympics above every other goal since I filled out that three-by-five-inch notecard at the OTC in Chula Vista as a starstruck sixteen-year-old. Now I knew exactly how hard it was to get there and the odds against making a third team; realistically, this might have been my last shot. I pushed that priority off the pedestal and decided Boston would become my beacon—a more worthwhile ambition at this point in my career. As an invitational race for elite runners, it had a process for picking athletes. No system was perfect, but there was more accountability if someone got caught doping. It was an iconic race for the masses as well, and my struggles had made me feel more of a kinship with "everyday" runners who toiled away with the aim of overall self-improvement rather than any specific time goal.

Letting the entire Olympic experience turn to dust would have been a mistake. I was really proud of the way I'd run in Rio and found I could separate that from what I knew about the field. I'd worked harder and been more patient than I'd ever thought was possible to make another team and get to experience the Olympic finish line. Being reasonable rather than coldly rational didn't always come easily to me, but I understood that I'd controlled everything I could control, and I allowed myself to feel the sense of redemption I'd been keying on since London. Natalie, Ryan, and I took a quick hop to Bariloche, Argentina, to indulge in the best ribeyes and Malbec wines in the region, then returned to Rio in time for me to march in the closing ceremony. It was the end of a four-year build, which can be a scary moment. We were all launching into the void of the unknown.

I took that concept one step further. Ryan and I celebrated our third wedding anniversary on our last day in Rio by buckling into hang-gliding harnesses and running off the edge of the Pedra da Gávea Mountain, putting our faith in the wings that lifted us higher and higher over the São Conrado neighborhood. As we got ready to push away from solid ground, we joked, "The couple that flies together dies together." Our senses were soon flooded by the thrill of seeing the sweeping panorama and singularly lush, majestic topography beneath us. It was a way to commit to the long view with all its risks, to open myself to reshaping a dream.

And if you ask me why you should bother to do that, I could tell you that the grave's a fine and private place, but none I think do there embrace. Nor do they sing there, or write, or argue, or see the tidal bore on the Amazon, or touch their children. And that's what there is to do and get it while you can and good luck at it.

Joan Didion, 1975 commencement address at University of California, Riverside

MILE 13

I FEEL SHALANE'S NUDGE and glance sideways. She's eyeing a row of portable toilets visible up ahead on one side of the course.

"Do you think it's okay to make a pit stop?"

This would be an unusual move for a contender. I'm not sure if Shalane is asking whether she'd be violating a race regulation or whether she wants my opinion on the strategic wisdom of taking a break. Either way, my answer is going to be the same. After our Olympic experience, I feel a sense of camaraderie with Shalane that doesn't exist with anyone else in the race.

"I think you're fine; we're going slow enough. I'll try and get to the front and slow it down."

That's all she needs to hear. She takes a diagonal to the shoulder of the road, turns right, and darts into the second closest toilet.

Mamitu Daska of Ethiopia has been antsy all morning

long, testing the field with surges, and she sees this as an opening to put her foot on the gas. It's emotional, not logical, given what it would take to solo into these headwinds for the entire second half of the race. Her move stretches out the pack, and in one instant, it becomes impossible for me to get to the front and try to dictate a slower pace as I told Shalane I would do. So I tap the brakes. I don't come to a full stop, just slow precipitously and look over my shoulder a few times to keep track of Shalane.

On one of those backward glances, I see another American, Serena Burla, wrestling with a trash bag that's flapping wildly in her hands. She had started in racing briefs and a bra top, and now has detoured to a garbage can to grab the bag and use it as a makeshift windbreaker. If I didn't know it before, this confirms it: Today is insane.

As the gap grows, I debate whether I've done the right thing, but I'm the one who told Shalane the pace was slow enough. I didn't promise I would wait, but now I feel obligated. I try to split the difference between her and the pack—the most efficient way to cover race moves without burning a match. Let the leader make a push, cut the distance by half, and slowly and patiently reel in the other half over a reasonable amount of road.

Shalane's rest stop is quick: just thirteen seconds. When she draws even with me, I point at my right shoulder and tell her to tuck in behind me. I'm happy to lead her back to the group.

Strangely, this is the first time I feel like I'm in the right rhythm for the conditions. Working in Shalane's service puts me in a more productive headspace. I'm focused on completing a task and no longer evaluating how I feel moment by moment. When she falls off my pace by a few yards, I decelerate just a touch. We're going to get back to the pack, chasing Daska together.

It takes us a few minutes to hitch onto the back of the group. When we get there, we find . . . ambivalence. Daska is thirty meters ahead, and nobody is quite willing to lead the charge to close that down. With about fifteen runners, by my count, we have the numbers for it. An organized effort could get the job done, but the field is too diverse: too many different nationalities, disparate talents, conflicting agendas. People make attempts here and there, stringing us out momentarily, then fall back, daunted by the task.

One of these surges leaves me behind, running—more like half jogging—alone on the black, rain-slicked road, its surface reflecting my blurry image back to me.

THE DEEPEST WELL

I WOKE MYSELF WITH a gasp: one big, sharp inhale.

Ryan didn't stir. Our bedroom was pitch-black and silent. The wind off Lake Michigan was absent, for once, and I didn't hear the usual rhythm of waves lapping at our shoreline.

I lay on my back and tried to process why I was awake when I had done nothing but sleep for weeks. There was no fragment of a nightmare floating in my mind, no pounding heart.

In fact, no heartbeat at all.

Fear surged through me. Had I woken up because I'd stopped breathing? I held completely still and listened for the reverb in my chest. Finally, I detected it, shallow and faint, alarmingly slow.

I was afraid to go back to sleep. I was afraid I wouldn't wake up.

My life didn't flash before my eyes. I didn't review the tailspin that had led to this night, how I had spiraled in a matter of months from one of the fittest people in the world to someone who struggled to climb a flight of stairs, my senses dulled, barely functioning. There was room for only one train of thought in my head.

I don't want to die. That's an improvement. At least I'm feeling something.

As I fought sleep, knowing I would lose, I made a decision.

If I wake up, I'll take the medication.

◆ ◆ ◆

THERE'S A VIVID snapshot in my mind of Josh talking to MK at the John Hancock postrace party a few hours after Boston 2017. The two of them are sitting in big red armchairs next to each other in a side room visible from the main room. He's leaning toward her, and his body language reads *intense*. It's obviously a lecture. I had a good idea of what he was saying, because I had expressed the same sentiment to her earlier that evening, a little more tersely: It was very possible I would never run here again.

This was the year I was going to win in Boston. I visualized it every day for months: fighting for the win down Boylston Street, breaking the tape, feeling the olive wreath placed on my head. I was very public about that goal and my confidence that I could achieve it. It felt as if everything had aligned, and everyone around me—my coaches, my sponsors, the media—kept reinforcing that. One friend was appalled that Natalie and I had booked a vacation in India right after the race. She suggested I might want to plan for the opportunities and obligations that went along with the title.

"You better have a refundable ticket," she said.

I shrugged it off: "I'll be the happiest person in the world if I have to cancel."

My concept of endurance included a lot more than lean muscle mass, high cardiovascular capacity, and mental staying power that left room for a finishing kick. It was about maintaining relentless forward progress, and I had done that. I'd dealt with only one major injury—the fractured femur—and failed to finish just once in my entire career. Otherwise, I hadn't run a single bad marathon. I had slowly worked my way back and finally surpassed my fitness level from the near-win in 2011. I was ready to validate the work of the last ten years. I felt due for a payoff.

Every step I'd taken since the London Olympics had been a step toward bridging the gap between runner-up and first on Boylston Street. Each training block had built on the last, each race had deepened my confidence. I hadn't backslid. The 2016 Olympic race had been a gut punch in terms of outcome—an especially sickening yet predictable one that continued to play out a few months later when gold medalist Jemima Sumgong was popped for erythropoietin (EPO), a drug banned because it stimulates production of oxygen-carrying red blood cells. Yet Rio had also shown me I was more fit than I'd been in five years. I was nailing workouts even after my Boston buildup was interrupted briefly by the flu. I was convinced I was going to be a little bit better than I'd ever been on this course.

And then it wasn't even close. Edna Kiplagat, running Boston for the first time and looking to add one more accolade to her already brilliant résumé, accelerated at Mile 18 and torched the field. She split 4:50 at Mile 20 and won by a full minute. Edna was Edna, and the fact that she landed on the top step of the podium wasn't a shock—the shock came from the way she demolished the rest of us.

What unfolded behind her was a surprise as well. I fully expected one of her two closest chasers to fall away: Rose Chelimo, from Bahrain, and Jordan Hasay. It was Rose's second marathon and Jordan's debut in the event. I followed my game plan precisely, splitting 1:12:33 in each half, knowing historically that should give me a shot in the last six miles. But no one faded. Instead, they powered away at a pace I had never experienced or witnessed before in the Newton hills, and I finished fourth.

I didn't register the whole picture until later; I couldn't afford to think negatively on the road. Even when things didn't seem to be falling my way at Mile 22 or 23 or 24, I had to keep pressing and stay in position to capitalize if my luck changed. I believed the race could pivot within instants if I caught someone going backward, and I knew how much ground I could make up even as late as the last few city blocks.

Reality hit me within a couple of hours. Nike athletes had swept both the women's and men's podiums. Both winners and three of the other four top finishers had worn the company's new Vaporfly shoes, which had been a mere rumor at the Rio Games the year before. They were said to improve running economy by as much as four percent, and other companies were scrambling to match the technology. "You finished second of the athletes without bouncy shoes," said one agent who sidled up to me afterward.

The well-meaning comment added to my sense that something had slipped through my fingers and a lot of my hard-earned knowledge had become irrelevant. Boston's unique course and the tactics it dictated had a hundred years of history. Not that any race was totally predictable, but there were certain patterns and trends I'd learned to count on. Was that all upended now? Had I just seen a turning point for how all marathons were run? Would Boston become indistinguishable from other races?

Jordan had run a 2:23, the fastest marathon debut for a US woman by almost three minutes. Galen Rupp finished second in the men's race. They were teammates at Alberto

Salazar's Nike Oregon Project—the group that had been under investigation for almost two years by the US Anti-Doping Agency for questionable medical practices.

ProPublica, a US-based investigative news organization, and the BBC collaborated to break the story in June 2015. Much of their reporting was based on interviews with two whistleblowers: Kara, who had ended her coaching relationship with Salazar in 2011; and former NOP assistant coach Steve Magness, who had left the group shortly afterward. Then everything went quiet for a while. *The Sunday Times* of London printed more details in early 2017, focused on Salazar's British distance star, Olympic gold medalist Mo Farah. On the eve of Boston, running insiders buzzed with speculation that the USADA's draft report had been leaked and another big media splash was imminent.

It was one more thing to add to a list of unsettling events in the months since Rio. Under international rules, Sumgong had been able to keep her Olympic title because her bust came afterward—even though this was her second offense. Fellow Kenyan Rita Jeptoo, winner of multiple majors, lost the last appeal in her own EPO case and was stripped of two titles. Ethiopia's Buzunesh Deba was elevated to first place at Boston 2014 more than two years after she crossed the finish line, and her time of 2:19:59 listed as the course record. Another Ethiopian, Mare Dibaba, was awarded the Chicago 2014 title. Old results in prestigious events kept getting reshuffled because of doping disqualifications, a trend that didn't look as if it would end any time soon. Some athletes, including Shalane and Kara, were in line for what were euphemistically called "upgraded" Olympic and world championship medals years later.

IN THE HOURS after the Boston 2017 finish, frustration and futility overwhelmed me. This race that was so very familiar to me suddenly felt foreign and uncomfortable. The swirling talk of tech shoes and speculation about borderline ethics made me feel as if I couldn't even really identify what I was up against.

I was thirty-three, and I'd never won a marathon. Maybe I needed to look for that somewhere else: a smaller-market race or a different event. Deep down, I still believed I was capable of winning a major, but continuing to chase that dream while competing against what felt like nefarious forces struck me as insanity. It seemed like time to readjust my expectations and where I chose to invest my energy.

I knew the Abbott World Marathon Majors were trying to keep elite fields clean and results believable. With prize money and credibility at stake, the WMM, organizers of the six biggest marathons in the world, including Boston, had instituted an additional drug testing program in 2015, but there was no foolproof system. If there were athletes exploiting the gray areas in anti-doping, I couldn't outwork or outsmart them. They were playing a different game. I questioned what I would learn about myself by racing them. It felt like a waste of valuable time and reignited my old college-era conflict about what I was doing with my life.

At the postrace Hancock event, I said some abbreviated version of all that to MK, one of few people I knew could comprehend how I felt. She didn't argue—or agree.

"We're at a party," she said. "The race literally just happened. We're not talking about this now."

I moved on, sipped my Moscow mule, tried to be civil. When I observed Josh venting to MK a little later, I appreciated how adamant he was being on my behalf, but I shared little of his energy. The way I saw it, my forward progress was blocked, and my window to win a major marathon had slammed shut. My 2011 stretch duel with Caroline Kilel, once so motivating, now loomed as a depressing reminder of what could have been. Overall, my sport seemed to be descending into disorienting chaos. It seemed easier to let go of ambition and stop caring.

Besides, I was about to leave for India.

♦ ♦ ♦

DESPITE LIVING THOUSANDS of miles apart, Natalie and I still formed a tight circle of two, always there for each other. Travel was a way of continuing to go against the grain of our upbringing. Dennis and Nancy were homebodies, to say the least. He had no interest in going places, and she was way too anxious to try. Natalie and I loved leaving our comfort zones to explore the big world and prove to ourselves that it wasn't all that scary. With a destination as far away as India, our approach was to go without telling them and share pictures when we got home.

I also regarded travel as continuing education: interludes where I left my running gear at home, ditched the one-dimensional self I had to be in training, and steeped myself in trying to learn something new. The idea of spending time in India dovetailed with my longtime intellectual curiosity about religion. I was baptized Methodist, but our family didn't practice or observe. I was fascinated with the power that faith could exert over people—sometimes for better, when it steered them toward kind acts, and sometimes for worse, as it did on 9/11, which coincided with my first few weeks in college. Eastern religion and philosophy intrigued me most of all. What they represented was less blind faith than mastery of self—or even renouncement of self. The benefits of that were obvious to me. I liked the idea of understanding how I fit into the world, appreciating how everything was interconnected but letting go of attachment and accepting change.

Natalie and I hired guides to take us all over northern India for twelve days, and we hit the ground running, spending a night or two in each place and traveling hours to the next stop on our itinerary. I lobbied hard to visit the holy city of Varanasi, teeming with the vibrancy of life yet also a revered site for end-of-life rituals. The contradictions engulfed our senses—nowhere more so than the river Ganges, a waterway that is both pure and polluted. We watched Hindu pilgrims flock to its banks for cremation ceremonies, casting ashes into the current upstream from where people bathe, wash their clothes, and brush their teeth. Sacred cattle roamed the streets, defecating at will. I was fascinated by how one of the world's oldest cities had endured the challenge of time and adapted without losing its identity or compromising its traditions. I inhaled the sights, sounds, and smells, challenging myself to absorb it all.

Yet the stimulation went only so far. I felt exhausted from the time we landed, numb to an extent that didn't make sense even when I factored in jet lag and postrace letdown. Instead of detaching and abandoning myself to an exhilarating adventure, I found myself mentally back on the Boston course, compulsively overthinking how the marathon had played out. I could focus on what was around me for a few hours, and then I'd zone out. Most tellingly, I seemed unable to be present enough to enjoy a couple of Kingfisher beers and some laughs with my sister.

As we were leaving our hotel in Varanasi, headed for Agra and the Taj Mahal, a guy came running after our car, yelling, "Ma'am! Ma'am! You forgot your wallet in the hotel!" Natalie and I stared at each other and then dug into our bags. I had my passport, but all my money was in the wallet.

I tried to remember when I'd last seen it. I hadn't put it in the safe. I hadn't set it on the counter. He handed it to me through the window, and I handed him back a few rupees, thinking, *What just happened?* I couldn't shake my confusion. The incident quickly assumed outsized importance in my mind.

I've been traveling since I was a teenager. It's not like me to lose track of my wallet. In India.

A profound fatigue flooded me from head to toe. I had the weird sensation of observing myself from a distance. *Not like me.* It didn't dawn on me that something deeper might be happening.

◆ ◆ ◆

WHEN JOSH BEGAN his formal conversations with MK about Boston 2018, she surprised both of us by bumping my appearance fee offer higher than it had ever been, without any of the usual negotiating. I took it as a gesture that acknowledged my consistent performances there and an indication that she still believed in me.

Now all I had to do was convince myself.

I took an unusually short break after Boston and jumped right back into training, trying to look at the road ahead, not behind. I told myself I'd run a strong race—again—and it was something to build on. Josh and I started sketching out the rest of the year and decided I might run Chicago that fall, but negotiations dragged on longer than we expected. At one point, he promised to get an offer to me the next day. Three days later, he called me back with a six-figure deal. "I don't care," I snapped. "You're late." I ruled out a fall marathon.

Impatience was my default mood as spring shifted to summer—bouts of irritability and negative thinking I normally wouldn't allow myself. It was the opposite of my mindset before Boston 2017, when everything seemed to be lining up ideally for me. Now even the most reliable parts of my life seemed complicated and enervating. The newest version of the Glycerin, my favorite Brooks training shoe, felt heavy and tight and made my routine runs miserable. I had to stop, adjust the laces, and stomp and shake my feet because they were going partially numb. The Glycerin had worked for me for years. *I'm getting blisters all over, the foam is not responsive, this is the best shoe ever, and they ruined it. I'm doing my job, why can't they do theirs?*

My training was solid, not great, but nothing in the segment clued me in to what was about to happen. I had entered the Gold Coast Half Marathon in Queensland, Australia, in early July, an atypical detour in my schedule. The goal was to crack a good one, put Boston in the rearview, and find a new way to progress. Kevin and I were banking on the flat course, ideal conditions, and my residual marathon strength to guarantee a morale booster. That strategy backfired when I finished in 1:12:15, more than two minutes off the personal best I was shooting for.

I stood in the cooldown area under brilliant sunshine, consumed with frustration. Kevin listened to me vent, sympathetic but as confused as I was. This felt like an inexplicable slump. I wasn't injured or in pain. My body just wasn't responding, and I couldn't put my finger on what was wrong. I was desolate, sure that I had wasted a massive chunk of my life chasing a ghost, accomplishing nothing of meaning.

I was also losing faith in the Hansons' ability to adapt their training philosophy and help me evolve and improve as an older runner. The brothers had shifted away from the founding concept of the ODP in a way that bothered me. When they added a marquee athlete such as Shadrack Biwott—whom I liked and respected personally—but didn't ask him to move to Michigan from California, contribute to group training, or even follow the training program, it made me feel as if we were teammates in name only. But we weren't talking about that or the news they were about to make.

My disenchantment turned to anger shortly after I got home from Australia, when I read—on Twitter—that the Hansons had signed veteran marathoner and former Nike Oregon Project athlete Dathan Ritzenhein.

Details from the leaked summary of USADA's

investigation into the group had finally seen the light in May, first reported by *The New York Times*. The document had been prepared for the Texas Medical Board, which was reviewing the actions of Dr. Jeffrey Brown, an endocrinologist affiliated with the NOP. The revelations of alleged violations and bending of anti-doping rules were both nauseating and infuriating, including the bombshell that Alberto had experimented with the use of supplemental testosterone on his own sons, who were not professional runners. The report also matched up with and confirmed the rumblings we'd been hearing for years. I limited myself to one snarky tweet on the subject in June, posting side-by-side images from news stories. The first showed Alberto gesticulating, wearing a backpack, under the headline "Two years and counting: the investigation into the Nike Oregon Project continues." The other was of a carrier pigeon nabbed by police for carrying a little pack filled with Ecstasy pills. My caption was: "But who wore it better?"

Dathan had cooperated with the investigation, and his name was all over the report. He'd given an extensive interview under oath to USADA about his six years with Alberto, during which he was often injured and in fear of having his Nike contract terminated or reduced. He told USADA that he'd started taking synthetic thyroid hormones at Alberto's urging to try to raise his testosterone level—even though nothing in his reported blood work outwardly suggested a need for that treatment. Dathan also received injections of L-carnitine, an energy-boosting amino acid that wasn't a banned substance but had been administered in doses that appeared to be over those allowed by anti-doping rules. Signing him two months after these details had become public blew my mind.

The Hansons had talked to me earlier in the year about their desire to bring on Dathan. He was from Michigan and they'd known him since he was a kid. I told them I thought that was great. I'd been a fan of his even before I witnessed his stellar 5,000 in Zurich back in 2009. Everyone liked Dathan, he would be a high-profile add to the group, and I was always inclined to give athletes the benefit of the doubt. But the revelations of the report changed everything, from my perspective. "Wow, lost a lot of respect for Dathan," I emailed Kevin. They never brought it up with me again. After I posted the double-backpack tweet, Kevin texted to let me know that one of my training partners thought it was "hilarious," but he didn't respond when I asked what Dathan thought. It was admittedly passive-aggressive on my part, but at least I was trying to start a conversation. I did reach out to Brooks for advice on how we were supposed to handle questions about Dathan and was told we would figure it out when it happened.

How could the Hansons proclaim they had zero tolerance for shortcuts and then sign someone who had flirted with ethical lines, from a group that was still under investigation? My take was that they were turning their backs on everything they had asked the team to believe in. Our communication began to break down at that point, but there was no big, dramatic rupture between me and Kevin and Keith. It was more like a hairline crack that widened, imperceptibly at first and then more obviously into a rift that couldn't be patched. And my inner pessimism clouded over any motivation I might have had to repair it at the time. I couldn't even run a decent half marathon, so what was the point?

Hard to say what I might have done if I hadn't had the prospect of a good payday in Boston. I committed to that deal in mid-July 2017 and told myself I had nine months to get myself ready. I didn't count on having to deal with the biggest blindside hit of my life.

◆ ◆ ◆

RELENTLESS FORWARD PROGRESS comes with a price. For most of my running life, I saw only one way to maintain momentum, and that was to take another step—right foot, left foot, repeat—especially when every cell in my brain and body was urging me to back off. I reasoned I had to do that to squeeze out the last iota of my potential and find out how good I really was. I dwelled on the rewards of that approach, not the risks, or how it might have to evolve along with me.

I may have grown up with the softened seasons of San

Diego, but Arizona State conditioned me to accept extremes. Sunrise brought soaring heat, making predawn workouts crucial; we got used to starting our naps when normal people were having their first coffee. We began the cross-country season in August, with temperatures well above one hundred degrees, and ended it with frost on the ground and a skim of ice on the puddles that formed on the track.

A cold front settled over Waterloo, Iowa, the week of the 2003 cross-country nationals—my junior year—sending temperatures into the teens with wind chill. Walt was adamant that we put it out of our heads. He hated the sympathetic stares we got when we walked around town in our team gear. It was common for an innocent spectator or fan to express sympathy for "poor Arizona State, dealing with this cold!" and it was equally common for Walt to suggest not so kindly where they could stuff it, because we knew how to manage adversity. His expectation was that we were going to be good, that we were going to run up to our ability level, that conditions weren't up for discussion.

"It doesn't matter how you feel," he would say. "It's whether you're ready or not."

That attitude helped me acclimate to Michigan winters, and it helped me shrug off weather anxiety on the eve of my marathon debut in 2007, when all anyone in Boston could talk about was the incoming nor'easter. Yet the most important adjustment I made in my first few years as a pro was adapting to fatigue. The Hansons' coaching philosophy was based on cumulative fatigue, training until we were dead tired, then staying in the well until we were comfortable there. I knew that other groups would pull out of that segment, do a mini-taper and a fitness-check race. We didn't. We lingered down there at the bottom and asked ourselves if we could dig even deeper.

I thrived on this for a long time. We were going to be the best at running hard when we were tired, and I was the fucking best of the best at managing that. When I felt the flu coming on in the middle of a training segment, I managed it. When I was beyond tired, I told myself it was exactly where I wanted to be. This was the unsexy part of the job: being so tired I fell asleep in my soup. The suffering was required for a chance at a payoff on race day.

Training was supposed to push me all the way to the brink—the breaking point right before I cracked. Racing was for finishing the job in front of an audience. Badassery thrived in the incremental space between wussing out and being an idiot. I reveled in finding that sweet spot. It gave me the confidence that I would persevere where others wouldn't or couldn't.

Of course I'm tired. This is a hard race. Everyone's tired.

I looked forward to the proving ground of the last six miles, where there was usually a clear choice. I could make the discomfort go away simply by slowing down. No one would call me out on it. Only I would know the truth—but then I'd have to look at the results afterward and live with the fact that I hadn't learned anything about myself. That I'd given up. The thought made me sick.

A decade at the top level of distance running had conditioned me to believe I was totally in charge of my mind-body connection. There's no way I could have become the endurance athlete I was without developing a skewed perception of fatigue and pain. If those sensations were like gradually deepening shades of color, I was blind to one whole end of the spectrum. I had never found it productive to dwell on regret or take part in blame games, but that baked-in habit of pushing through didn't serve me well when I dismissed the deep itch that turned out to be a broken leg, or five years later, when different warning signs began to flash.

◆ ◆ ◆

"WE'RE GOING THROUGH an absurd amount of Drano," Ryan said to me one day that summer. Clumps of hair pulled loose in my hands every time I took a warm shower, something I found myself doing automatically two or three times a day because I felt cold all the time. My legs tingled, and my feet kept falling asleep—as they had in the buildup for Australia—even when I wasn't running. Could that really be all down to the shoe? My training log, usually hard evidence of inspiration, started to resemble Swiss cheese, with more holes than substance. My mysterious lack of motivation and the way I was laboring through recovery runs made me wonder if I might be iron deficient, and I got some blood work done.

Mostly, I was convinced I had to be allergic to our new golden retriever puppy. It was the only big change in my surroundings. We'd lost Miles earlier that year, and Atlas was inconsolable—it was hard to watch him searching the house. Ryan didn't want to wait long to get him a buddy and make us a two-dog household again. He'd gone to Wisconsin to pick up the puppy after I came back from Australia, and named him Boston. His idea. I felt too worn out to suggest something else. Within a few days of having Boston constantly rubbing against my arms and legs and face, begging to play and generally being obstreperous, my eyes dried out and itched constantly, and I felt short of breath. I had zero practice at feeling this bad for no discernible reason. It was unnerving, and I felt myself becoming combative.

Our friend Reid Buchanan was running a mile race in Charlevoix. Ryan invited him to stay with us and tack on a few days of training afterward. The catch was that Ryan, who was competing in triathlons as a high-level amateur, was about to take off for a ten-day training camp in Hawaii.

It was bad timing, leaving the four of us together: Reid, who had retriever-level drive himself; the exuberant, oblivious puppy; Atlas, who hated nearly everyone; and me, who definitely hated everyone at that juncture. Verbally jousting with Reid was usually a favorite pastime of mine on training runs, but I didn't have the energy or sense of humor for debates, so, instead, I sniped at him, "Shut up. I don't care."

When Reid's training stint ended, I drove him to Detroit Metro Airport, four hours south. I'd been going back and forth between Charlevoix and Rochester for years by then, but even this routine trip suddenly felt like a massive effort. I had to keep the radio on high volume and the AC on full blast to keep myself from nodding off at the wheel. *I shouldn't be driving,* I thought, and actually pulled over to nap on the way back. When I got home, I put Boston in his crate and crashed. It was my thirty-fourth birthday, and I spent most of it either sleeping or crying. I didn't know why I was so sad, and I had no interest in figuring it out.

I WENT BACK downstate again for a scheduled workout with Kevin. He asked me how I'd been doing since Australia, and I told him a very condensed version of the truth: not good. My training runs had been a minute per mile slower than usual yet seemed significantly more difficult. I had put on weight while building up mileage, which didn't make sense. He rattled off the prescribed session, a simple progression run to gauge where I was at: "Six-mile workout, super easy, start at six-minute pace for two miles and build into it."

I started crying. Kevin was a little stunned. So was I.

"You don't have to do it," he said.

"I think I should. I need to get back in shape."

That's what I said out loud. Inwardly, the thought that I might not be able to execute a simple workout completely flustered me. I couldn't stomach another disappointment. After years of being hungry to learn and know what was next, I didn't want to discover that the magic I'd always found in running, the inner light of talent and self-belief, could be ebbing away. I was mentally running alongside my former self and getting dropped.

My fears materialized as soon as I started. Right foot, left foot, no rhythm. First mile: 5:59. I couldn't breathe. Second mile: 6:20. No way would I be hitting any splits.

We stopped the workout. "Go home," Kevin said. "I don't know what's wrong, but something is clearly not right. Let us know when the blood work comes in."

I got the results later that day. The level of the muscle enzyme creatine kinase (CK) in my blood was off the charts: 900, when the usual range is below 100. My iron level seemed fine, and my white blood cell count was a little low. I forwarded the numbers to John Ball, who was in Canada.

"Did you have a hard workout?" he wrote back.

Yeah, no.

Back in Charlevoix, I huddled under a pile of blankets on the couch, freezing in early August and brain-fogged, with zero attention span or ability to concentrate. I was attempting to read the novel *A Gentleman in Moscow* but couldn't hold the book upright. My arms, shoulders, and neck were leaden, and the effort of sitting up was exhausting. I'd wake up to find the book on the floor in front of me.

I felt as if I were on a dimmer switch being dialed down by some unseen hand, watching it happen from the one lucid corner of my mind, a hostage powerless to change it. *This is who I am now. I don't have any motivation to be better. I don't want to be a nicer person. I just want to stay in bed.* I wasn't consciously suicidal, but I also didn't care if I woke up.

Ryan had been pestering me to eat since he'd come back from Hawaii, only to watch me doze off at the table. I kept telling him I had to be allergic to the puppy. The first week of August, his concern peaked.

"You can't walk up a flight of stairs," he said. "You have to go see someone."

I was beyond being combative. The next day, Ryan drove me to the Urgent Care clinic in nearby Traverse City, where a doctor saw me, took my information, and ordered a blood panel.

The voice mail message came in hours later: "You have severe hypothyroidism."

I called Kevin, as promised. I laughed when I told him

the diagnosis, and I knew he would appreciate why. I was convinced that hypothyroidism was a buzzword, a trendy diagnosis especially prevalent in my sport, and the USADA investigation had only confirmed that. "This wasn't even on my radar," I said. "There's no family history. I don't even know where my thyroid is." Kevin was concerned but thought Urgent Care wasn't the most reliable source, and he suggested I get a second opinion.

Ryan and I did some searching and found a family practice in Elk Rapids, Michigan. It was reputable and, more important, could get me in immediately. The next day, I was ushered into an exam room. A nurse practitioner walked in. I was righteously indignant.

"They called me yesterday and said I had a thyroid problem, and I want to get a real opinion, not Urgent Care."

"Urgent Care called you?" she said, sounding surprised. "They don't call anybody unless it's an emergency. Do you have your blood work? I'll go check and see what's going on."

She wasn't gone for long. Her face was lined with concern when she came back.

"You need to get on meds yesterday," she said. "I'll send in the prescription for seventy-five micrograms of Synthroid." She paused, looked at me, and adjusted. "I'm going to write it for a hundred twenty-five."

The prescription was for synthetic thyroid hormone, an irony that struck me with almost palpable force. The brand name, Synthroid, rang out like a four-letter word. In my mind, thyroid medication was a shortcut drug, something athletes had sought out or been instructed to take with no true medical need.

I felt a flash of fear, subsumed swiftly by anger that boiled down to a single obstinate word: no.

"No way," I said out loud. "Not doing that."

The nurse practitioner regarded me with a mixture of compassion and exasperation.

"You're welcome to seek another opinion from an endocrinologist, but your body's thyroid hormone levels are so low that if you don't start taking the medication now, you'll be in a coma, or dead, before you can get an appointment," she said. "Your muscles are breaking down, your liver is being damaged, there's a good chance your cholesterol is high. Your body is prioritizing the essentials, and everything else is shutting down. That's why you're sleeping so much. I'll send the prescription in. You must feel horrible."

"I can't just take whatever," I said. "I get drug tested. I need a therapeutic-use exemption." I was flailing, *and* I was wrong. Thyroid medications didn't require a TUE—that was likely why they had become so popular in sports.

"Do whatever you need to," she said. "I'll fill out whatever paperwork you need. You have to get on this now, or you're going to die. You don't have time to get to a specialist before this becomes serious."

I still wasn't buying it. How many years had I been

pushing my limits? I would get through this. I always had. Bones knit back together. Bodies recovered.

It doesn't matter how I feel.

Of course I'm tired. Everyone's tired.

Wasn't it possible I just needed more rest? I couldn't remember the last time I'd taken as much as an ibuprofen. Now I was being told I'd have to be on medication for the rest of my life, by people who had known me for all of one day. *This* medication, with all its controversial baggage? Wouldn't people think I was a hypocrite?

Nothing much had made sense to me recently in my constant state of depletion, this least of all. How could I be dying when I had as much endurance as any athlete in the world? I went to bed still resisting the notion and sank immediately into my usual deep-water sleep. Until the middle of the night, when my survival instinct kicked in, and I surfaced, gasping for air.

◆　◆　◆

I STARTED TAKING the medication the next morning and waited to see what would happen. At first, my body's thermostat remained wildly off. I swaddled myself in a jacket and blankets on the couch and avoided interacting with our neighbors when they came over to hang out with Ryan. It took about a week before I noticed any change.

Sensation—heat and the slow pulse of blood flow—returned to my hands and my face. Slowly, I got stronger. The day I walked upstairs without feeling winded was cause for celebration, but also signaled the total rebuild that lay ahead.

I was still fragile and flattened when the World Championships started in London, and dozed on and off for most of the women's marathon coverage. But I watched the last six miles fully tuned in as my old friend Amy—now Amy Hastings Cragg—hung tough in a lead group of four. Emotions rolled through me with the force of actual waves as I rooted for her to hunt down that dream we'd both wanted forever. The women who had finished one-two in Boston switched places, as Rose Chelimo eventually outkicked Edna Kiplagat for the win. Amy sprinted for third, finally rewarded with a medal for all those years of hard work—some of which we'd done together. It was validating to see her compete with the best in the world. It brought back that bold, youthful take we had on our shared long runs: *Why not us? Why not me?* I was thrilled, yet found the excitement exhausting and slept for the rest of the day.

I had to reconcile the fact that I wasn't bulletproof, that I needed to get well, that taking medicine didn't confer an advantage in the sense I had always thought of as cheating. It would simply treat very real and serious symptoms. The realization was humbling and illuminating. My diagnosis made me take responsibility for my health.

As the mental fog lifted, I studied my thyroid levels and tried to understand where I had been and where I needed to be. The blood level of thyroid-stimulating hormone (TSH) told how well the thyroid was functioning, and thyroxine (free T4) was the hormone produced by the thyroid. A normal TSH would have been 0.45 to 5.33 uIU/mL (micro-international units per milliliter of blood). Mine was measured at >92. A normal free T4 was 0.7 to 2.0 ng/dL (nanograms per deciliter of blood), and mine came in at <0.2. My constellation of symptoms had a name: severe hypothyroidism. I read more and learned that if I'd gone untreated much longer, my body's vital systems would have continued to decay, leading to a severely altered mental state and even unconsciousness, clinically known as myxedema coma.

I also realized that my thyroid issues had been brewing probably for at least a year, maybe longer. I would get a sore throat or lose my voice out of nowhere, or feel what I thought was the flu taking hold. I'd rest, it would pass, and I'd move on without noticing the pattern. Still, I wondered how I could have seen myself in the mirror in the late stages—my swollen eyes, the missing outer third of my eyebrows, the skin on my face forming folds like a Shar-Pei's from retaining water—and not understood how much trouble I was in. Tolerating what most people would consider intolerable is the flip side of endurance. I couldn't wish that out of myself, but I could take the mindset and discipline I used as armor and channel them toward something more sustainable.

I needed a new template to continue progressing. I was a different person and a different athlete than I'd been two or five or ten years before. I didn't want the extra stressor of annual trips to altitude anymore. I didn't want to go back to the workout schedule rooted in cumulative fatigue that I knew the Hansons would send me, and I didn't want any part of their revamped team. Ryan and I loved our lives in Michigan, and we had zero desire to relocate for me to join another group. I was going to have to construct my own way forward and my own way to gauge progress.

There's a reason that most relationships in sport don't last forever, but I hadn't anticipated splitting with Kevin and Keith. At a press conference just the year before, I had said, "I'm going to finish my career with these guys. I'm never going to be with a different coach. It's worked super well. We're always on the same page." There were just too many reasons to turn that page now.

I knew all of that would be irrelevant if I didn't have a future in running, which seemed murky at best. I had the financial base—a long-term Brooks contract and the Boston 2018 deal locked in—but my health situation would take a while to reset. On many days, I doubted whether I had enough time or patience to get myself in top form by the third Monday in April, but I restrained the impulse to make any big decisions. I didn't run a single purposeful step in August and September, and resolved to let my motivation and interest steer me. *When I miss running, I'll start running again. No rush.* I spent long, peaceful hours kayaking and fishing, trying to define my own happiness. I kept my condition private and let the public and media think it was a mental health break.

When I started training again, I tried to keep in mind that I was rehabbing from more than a stress fracture. Getting in shape after the broken femur was straightforward, if tedious. It was a matter of putting in time and seeing the logical return on that investment. By comparison, up against something systemic and invisible such as thyroid levels, I faced a new mini-mystery every day. I didn't know when and how I'd get knocked down. I wasn't sure about my next steps as I tried to piece together a workout and race schedule that would get me ready to run respectably in Boston. I looked for shorter races where there would be few to no expectations freighted on me. In November 2017 I flew east for the New York Road Runners' 5k event that ends at the NYC Marathon finish line in Central Park, but deliberately left the city the day before the big event. I was still too raw and disillusioned to spend much time around industry people, and the slow estrangement from the Hansons had begun to affect my all-important relationship with Brooks.

Josh had forwarded me a message from then–Brooks

Sports Marketing manager Steve DeKoker that read, "Between you and me, we know that Desi has had some tension with Kevin—none of my business—however, I want to stress the importance of her relationship with the Hansons going forward. Brooks sees Desi as a Hansons-Brooks team member and a product of years of good coaching from them. Any dissension between the two only hurts our long-term relationship with either Desi or the Hansons. We hope they will continue to be supportive of each other." Message received. I felt I was being viewed as a Hansons product, not an individual athlete, but I also sensed it was in my best interests to pretend outwardly that things were fine—or there could be consequences.

My only curiosity about NYC was how Shalane would do, coming back from injury. She was the top US woman in the race, but, as usual, given the drought that now stretched back to the 1970s, she wasn't the favorite. I had come a long way in my view of her, from competitive antipathy to admiration. We hadn't crossed paths since that deflating yet bonding moment after the race in Rio; she'd been struggling with back problems, so between that and my thyroid condition, one or the other of us had been sidelined. Sure, she was a rival, and I badly wanted the chance to test myself against her again. But now, with more maturity, I also regarded her as a teammate—not just because we'd competed in the same colors at the Olympics but because we had pushed each other and our peers to be better, to refuse to let ourselves be haunted by past disappointments, to get to a place we might not have reached on our own. We had a mutual, well-earned respect.

In a pre-NYC media conference call, Shalane had spoken out about the Salazar case in a way I appreciated. She was responding to a question about Galen Rupp and Jordan Hasay, who had finished first and third in their respective races in Chicago the month before. "That program, the NOP, has been under investigation for the last two years," she said. "So as a fan of my own sport, it's hard to have full excitement and faith when you don't know all the facts yet. There's still an investigation going on, so it's hard to truly and genuinely get excited about the performances that I'm watching."

I sent Shalane a good-luck text early on race morning. She was on the bus to the start and answered with a joke. I knew how laser serious she was before a big event, and her relaxed tone got my attention. *She's in a good headspace,* I thought, and told Ryan so. I'd had no intention of watching, but on a hunch, I changed my mind and turned on the television. A little more than two hours later, I sat riveted, my eyes welling up with emotion, as Shalane distanced the rest of the field in Central Park and ran solo for the last three miles. I flashed back to 2009, when she hadn't yet run a marathon and came to New York to check out the event. She and I had watched Meb win together from our VIP perch in the back of the press truck; now she was about to join him on the list of champions. I could see her gaining conviction and getting stronger as she closed out the race. I reached for my phone and tapped out a Tweet.

> In tears. Thank you @ShalaneFlanagan for giving us something to believe in. Congratulations!

SECONDS BEFORE SHALANE hit the tape, becoming the first American woman to win NYC in forty years, she fist-pumped and yelled, "Fuck yeah!" Her fierce, joyous outburst marked the end of an era of frustration for our entire generation. Sure, we'd been outrun at times. We'd also been robbed—a lot. And mostly, we'd been discounted for so long. It was motivating to see someone I had raced with, and believed in, have her moment. It restored some of my faith—open-eyed faith—in the world of running. It gave me a sliver of hope that it would be worth it to keep hoisting myself, hand over hand, out of the deep well of fatigue.

RIGHT FOOT, LEFT *foot, repeat.* There was no other way to begin to move forward again, but now that I had chosen to go back to work, I also had to redefine what progress meant to me, how to make it lasting. It was no coincidence that I would gravitate to a holy site such as Varanasi or a revered race like Boston, both rich with tradition but continually adapting. That was how places and people endured. It was the capacity to be dynamic, to evolve and reinvent, that kept them alive, and I wanted to build that into running. I needed the comfort of familiar rhythms—digging down, finding my limits—combined with the possibility of change. Maybe hitting the purest groundwater didn't require drilling through quite so much rock.

MILE 17

I'M OFF THE back, separated from the pack, but my mind isn't on that gap or on race tactics. I'm focused on the practical aspects of how deep into the race I should go. I've made it past the halfway mark, which helps me feel the attempt was worth the effort; otherwise, I would have felt exposed as unprepared. Now I have another choice to make.

My mind ticks through the variables, one by one. Physically, I know I'm okay. Nobody that Shalane and I peeled off after her bathroom stop is bridging back to catch me. Logistically, it's very difficult to get back to the Fairmont from here. I'd have to wait for the race van to pick me up, or try to get an Uber, or take the T. And even in the absence of near-hurricane conditions, moving around Boston during the marathon is impossible.

Stopping, standing still, or walking any distance in my drenched clothes, letting the chill penetrate to my bones, unappealing options at the moment. Continuing has its own risks, which I know only too well after having clawed my way back to health for the last year. What would running the full distance do to my body? Would it sink me back down into a well of fatigue? How long would it take me to recover? These are the hypotheticals that John Ball and I have been mulling over for months. Now I'm left to make the decision in real time.

Running is the best way, the fastest way, the most pragmatic way to get to the finish. My mind circles back to London, where the Olympic course made it easy: The first two miles were a loop. I stepped off where I started. Unlike that day, I'm physically able to keep going. The gap hasn't been extended too far. I'm watching the race from behind, and I feel fine. I see Molly Huddle at the front. I can tell the lead to Daska is stretching out. If they don't chase her down now, she'll run away with the race.

I decide to dig in to close the gap. I'll head to the front of the group, push into the wind, and get them to the leader. That will keep me warm, and I can easily jog in from there or when I feel I've given enough to the chase group. It's a spoiler's role, and it'll keep me busy for a little while, which will be better than dwelling on the potential misery of the remaining miles.

I abandon any idea of a plan and start improvising.

After I rejoin the pack, I head to the front, passing Shalane, who's yo-yoing off the back. As I press the pace, I again feel like I'm in the right rhythm for the day. The stretch gives way to the steepest downhill on the course, where people always let loose. It's far enough along in the race that moves can be real.

I peek back to see if Molly is tucked in on my shoulder, but she's ten meters behind me. Again, I've created separation, and not just with one or two runners. The chase pack has splintered. I don't know what the rest of the race might hold, but the optics of this moment could save my career. I've made it look as if I haven't lost a step. It's well before the real racing should begin, but on the television screen, I'll look like I'm a contender.

As we head down to the quaint burg of Newton Lower Falls—the steepest descent on the course—I let the downhill pull me into a quicker cadence. I'm thinking tactically. Gladys Chesir and I take turns leading into the wind. Her white Nike windbreaker billows in the wind, emphasizing her slight frame. She's relatively new to the marathon, and I don't know much about her. At times, she seems intent on reeling in Daska as quickly as possible. It's the wrong effort at the wrong time, in my mind—too early. This is a challenging part of the race. The I-95 overpass is the first real sustained climb on the course, and I think of it as the first true Newton hill, even though most people count only the three after the fire station. Grabbing fluids, drinking them, and covering moves are all tough to manage. Behind me, Edna Kiplagat, last year's winner, is fighting to hang on.

Something shifts when I sense I've dropped her. It's a reflexive, involuntary realization: I'm in the mix, however inadvertently.

I make the right-hand turn at the Newton fire station a few steps behind Chesir. She's put some distance on me, but she hasn't buried me. I keep my eyes trained on her back. Maybe I can run her down and grab another second-place finish in Boston. That wouldn't be a bad outcome, considering where this workday started.

I can't drop out now.

THE RIGHT WHY

NATALIE AND I navigated through the narrow streets of central Rome, minding our footing on the cobblestones, to reach what a map and intuition told us was the best place in the city to run. A flight of steps led us down to a bike path along the river Tiber. Natalie took off on her easy run. Traffic noise evaporated as I eased into a quality session of 8 × 3 minutes at half-marathon pace, or roughly 5:15 per mile, with 2 minutes of jog recovery. Each 3-minute segment gave me a chance to turn over my legs at a higher cadence and reacquaint myself with the speed that used to come naturally. I appreciated the beauty and novelty of my surroundings: The flat water of the Tiber mirrored high, curving stone walls softened by trailing ivy, the trees above, and the arched bridges. As the session progressed, my body felt more fluid working at a quicker pace. I was in my element, training alone, yet in the company of people sharing in the ritual of exercise. Cyclists wheeled around me on the path, and a handful of others nodded or gave a quick wave in the universal language of runners.

When I decided to give professional running a shot after college, Frank Browne offered me great advice. "Read and travel as much as you can," he said. "You'll never have more free time to do this in your adult life, until you retire." Frank had taken me seriously from early on, and I returned the favor. His words came back to me as I was trying to design a program that would help me move forward with the same high competitive aspirations, pursued with a new, intentionally broader approach. I could take a watch and running shoes anywhere, and I'd always tried to carve out extra time for travel experiences wherever I ran. During my second training stint in Kenya, I took a side trip with Olympian Diane Nukuri to her home country of Burundi and later detoured to the Masai Mara game reserve, joined by MK and Natalie, for a photo safari.

By now, my sister and I had run and explored together on every continent except Antarctica, and we were still hungry for more. That was the logic behind planning a two-week trip to Rome and Marrakesh in November 2017. I wasn't in post-marathon break mode, as I usually was that time of year. This wasn't a running-centric trip like Kenya or a dedicated vacation like India. It was a hybrid, an opportunity to see if I could soak in the cities and culture while balancing the demands of training as I attempted to get myself ready for a winter racing schedule.

Since I was no longer operating within the rigid structure of the team, I could train however I wanted, whenever I wanted. My first priority was to build in more rest. I slept later, untethered from a strict eight o'clock start time. I scheduled more days between hard sessions to make sure I was fully recovered, departing from the standard two-day interval I had grown used to. Within each workout, I gave myself the option to adjust pace, effort, or volume of quality work depending on how strong I felt. I would shoot for a session to be between six and nine miles of quality work, ranging from a 5k or 10k race pace to a marathon pace.

I needed to find out if I was intrinsically motivated enough to put in the work when I was in charge and no one was watching. If I skipped a day or week of running, nobody would know, comment, or be invested. If I bailed when a session began to get difficult, I was accountable only to myself. I'd always had an easy answer for *How badly do I want this?* Unearthing the reasons behind that desire and taking them with me every day was a more complicated endeavor.

We ran along the river Tiber every morning and spent our afternoons sampling amazing wine and touring the marvels of the Colosseum and the Vatican. In Marrakesh, we walked the Jemaa el Fna marketplace and took in the Yves Saint Laurent museum, feasted on lamb tagine and sipped mojitos made from the famously sweet Moroccan mint. By the time we boarded the flight home, I was convinced I could weave detours like this into my schedule and maintain my discipline—in fact, possibly improve it. I was more than capable of doing a workout that ended without someone nodding in approval or shaking their head in dismay. The work would be the same whether I was running through one of the world's ancient capitals or on the dirt roads of northern Michigan. Keeping myself curious and engaged—and at least mildly amused—seemed increasingly like the key to my professional well-being.

◆ ◆ ◆

MORNINGS BACK IN Charlevoix, layered up against the deepening cold, I pushed the door open, put my head down, and got down to business on routes I knew by heart. It was a conscious act of commitment every time. Getting back in shape is never easy, but, as I kept reminding myself, being in shape is awesome. And for all my aversion to monotony, once I settled back into routine, I thrived on it. The structure freed me to do other things. "The grind" meant something positive to me: a challenge to embrace repetition and approach it creatively. It annoyed me when I heard "the grind" used in a pejorative way. Sure, it could be tedious, but it was a choice. Go off and do something else if you hate it.

There were only so many hours I could spend running, and the rest of my workday sounded pretty good by comparison to most: I napped. I got massages. I took Atlas and Boston out to play in the snow. I read voraciously—often a couple of books a week. Some evenings, Ryan and I sipped bourbon by the fireplace. Always neat to start, adding a little water or ice to open it up in the glass later on.

Bourbon had been a longtime pleasure for me, and not a guilty one, just part of defining my own conventional wisdom. We had started sampling bourbon with our friends when we were first dating, bargain hunting selectively at Costco. Sitting around and comparing bottles was a fun social thing, but I got more and more curious about what went into making them taste the way they did. My teammates created a Wikipedia page for me that included the phrase "other interests: collecting whiskey and tapestries." The information went mainstream, reporters quizzed me about it, and fans sent me bottles and loved to connect over whiskey stories. (I received some tapestries as well, but never had the heart to disclose that part had been a joke.) I was sparing about consumption during my most intense training blocks, but I also didn't believe in putting up rigid guardrails. I enjoyed busting the myth that distance runners had to live like monks 365 days a year.

As I logged miles in rolling farmland or the flatter stretches near Lake Michigan, I learned there was at least one way I had to change my routine. For most of my career,

I hit my splits, forcing a bit if I needed to, then tilted my left wrist, glanced at my watch, and saw exactly what I expected. If I had an off day, it generally wasn't an unsolvable mystery—I'd figure it out. Because I was still recovering, I had to put aside the philosophy of cumulative fatigue ingrained in me in my years with the Hansons: *It doesn't matter if you're tired. Do the mileage you're supposed to do. That's what prepares you.* Now I had to structure my training around the exertion that was rational day by day, rather than an exact number of miles assigned to me. Gauging workouts by relative effort—*How do I feel?*—was foreign territory for me. It called for more decision-making on the fly.

On any given day, I'd think, *I feel decent, I should extend this.* Or, *This feels like diminishing returns, I need to shut it down.* Or, *This feels right, even though the clock says something that it shouldn't.* I mostly ran alone, but Ryan came along sometimes to get in his own workout. We'd talk afterward, but he understood my state of flux and didn't weigh in on the distance or the quality of what I'd done. He respected the fact that he wasn't my coach and did what he always did: listen and be emotionally supportive.

Next, I needed to put together a schedule that would prepare me for Boston. I circled April 16, 2018, on the calendar and started to work backward. I would run the New York City Half Marathon in March, a standard part of my build in recent years. By then, I thought there was a more than

decent chance I'd feel closer to a hundred percent and post
a result that would confirm I was on the right trajectory. In
a departure from my typical Florida training segment, I decided to spend February and part of March training in Arizona and working with John Ball. Searching for a
competitive environment that would be novel, low-stress,
and enjoyable, and inspired by my experience in Rome, I
entered three short, early winter events in Europe: one on
cobbles and two on grass. Running different distances on
different surfaces against unfamiliar fields would avoid
comparisons to past results and give me the chance to race
into shape without necessarily exposing that I wasn't in
prime condition.

Mainly, I wanted to put the intrinsic pleasure of running
front and center. I knew this marathon block wouldn't resemble what I'd done before. It was fine to lay it all out on
paper, but I was well aware that I couldn't be overly attached
to it. I would have to shift and adjust as I went.

◆ ◆ ◆

I PUT 2017 in the rearview on New Year's Eve by running
the 5k BOclassic in Bolzano, Italy, at the foot of the Dolo-
mite Mountains. The course starts in the main town piazza
and loops around on cobblestone streets through the heart
of the city. It was a laid-back start for my new season, since

my finishing time was irrelevant: In twenty-degree temperatures, on a bumpy, twisting route, no one would expect to
be particularly fast. I put in my sixteen minutes, and that
evening, Ryan and I went out and toasted the occasion with
a few British athletes, including Andy Vernon and Steph
Twell, who had performances worth celebrating. It seemed
like an auspicious way to turn the page.

The Campaccio, a cross-country race outside Milan the
next weekend, didn't play out as well. I couldn't lock into
the right pace for a 5k and finished behind people who had
no business beating me. My joints were aching, hindering
my stride, and I was struggling to breathe deeply, an unwel-
come reminder of the previous summer. That only got
worse in the Great Edinburgh Cross Country race in Scot-
land, held on a true cross-country course, hilly and rugged.
I had to labor to avoid coming in last. Embarrassed and exhausted, I applied bourbon to my wounded confidence,
venting to a fellow runner at the bar. I hadn't progressed on
this European trip—in fact, my fitness had declined. My
knee was swollen. I hadn't been able to inhale and exhale
normally for a week.

My intentions had been good, and smart, or so I'd
thought. I'd done all the right things: taken medication appropriate to my diagnosis, given myself ample rest, built
slowly, and mixed things up by mapping out an alternative
winter season to refresh my motivation. The old equation—

plan logically, work hard, get results—seemed to be failing me. It was disheartening. Would I ever get back to where I was? Did my treatment need to be adjusted? Or had I expected too much too soon? Despite my resolve to stay in the present, I couldn't help questioning the basic premise of what I was doing. Just how fixable was this?

Am I done? Why should I keep trying?

Boston, a little more than three months away, was suddenly the next major event on my schedule. The elite fields had been announced, the women's race would feature perhaps the deepest American talent ever, and I felt pressure to measure up. It was a multigenerational group, ranging from Deena, still one of the people I admired most in the sport, to Jordan Hasay, who was widely expected to land on the podium again. Shalane would be there, of course, the reigning New York champion taking another shot in her hometown, along with contenders such as Molly Huddle and Serena Burla. I wasn't going to line up in Hopkinton if I didn't think I could put in a credible effort or if that effort would erode the fragile toehold on health I'd gained in the last few months. I needed help managing my predicament from someone I trusted, and who fully understood my situation and the demands of my profession.

I also needed warm weather, familiar roads, and a setting that might help reinforce the reasons to try. All of those things would be waiting for me in Arizona.

◆ ◆ ◆

JOHN AND I met in his private office in Chandler, out of earshot of the treatment room, where other clients were coming and going. I knew he would be honest. He was concerned that I still had visible swelling around my eyes and in my neck, remnants of my worst hypothyroidism symptoms. He saw what a hard time I was having getting deep breaths in and out. I told him I felt tightness in my chest, as if I could use only the top third of my lungs. "I think you broke a rib at some point," he said. Whatever the cause, I had lingering respiratory weakness.

With a thyroid condition like mine, treatment was a process that couldn't be rushed. My body needed time to adjust to the medication, and I had blood tests done every six weeks to see if I was on the right track. I also was scheduled to have a thyroid ultrasound and an MRI of the pituitary gland at the base of the brain to make sure there weren't any other underlying issues. John started working on managing my breathing, but one of his biggest rehab and repair jobs was on my psyche, still shaken after the letdown of my European racing segment. He kept reminding me that this recovery was not going to include a lot of instant gratification.

"Think of this as an injury," he said. "It's going to be a long climb back. There are going to be ups and downs along the way."

When we talked about whether I'd be fully ready for Boston, John was pragmatic as he spelled out what he saw as my options. "If you want to compete at a high level for more than another year or two, you need to take your time getting back to full health," he said. "You can't force it, and you probably shouldn't run Boston. If you don't care about the long term, we can get you ready now and cash in on the short-term opportunities." We covered that ground in conversation a number of times over the next month as I chipped away at the training, and we both knew the NYC Half would be pivotal to my decision-making.

I was in Scottsdale, staying with Reid Buchanan in an apartment the Mammoth Track Club had rented for him. He didn't mind training alone but was happy to have my company. Early on in my recovery, I'd called him to apologize for how I'd acted when he was training in Charlevoix. We had a legitimate bond despite that hiccup in our relationship, and he was an ideal roommate for me at the time. I was starting to understand what kind of support I needed, and liked the notion of creating a sense of team that ran deeper than wearing the same jerseys.

Ryan and I had first met Reid when I was training in Mammoth Lakes the year before, and we'd all connected immediately. He was from Kansas, a lanky guy in his midtwenties with a shock of blond hair and a big smile. He was still excited about the sport and had a different attitude from some other younger runners I'd been around. He liked debating and could come off as abrasive, yet I could tell that his zeal for arguing was often just another way to pick my brain. Reid had genuine curiosity about my experiences, wanted to learn from them, and appreciated the chance. I felt like a bit of a mentor to him; it was rewarding to know that someone else could benefit from my hard-won knowledge.

Now he was seeing me head off to appointment after appointment, and he wanted to know if I was okay. I assured him that I was, and we resumed our usual nitpicking banter on subjects ranging from the comedic brilliance of Bo Burnham, to the meaning of the lyrics in Gucci Mane's "Both," to the value of summer racing in Europe versus racing on the road.

I found comfort in old routes: Tempe Town Lake, Papago Park, and the Crosscut Canal, where strings of baby ducks paddling behind their mothers signaled the arrival of spring. The vast, bold paint strokes of Arizona sunsets lit up my evening runs. I had forgotten how a certain percentage of Tempe runners ran in tights and long sleeves when it was forty degrees, and laughed inwardly, remembering how I was that person when I was at ASU; moving to Michigan taught me what real winters were like. Arizona was a stable, familiar environment that grounded me at a time when everything else seemed to fluctuate day to day, following no detectable pattern. I worked to reframe my daily purpose, gambling that if I pushed through the subpar days and didn't let them get into my head, it would pay off when, or if, I got myself totally right.

My best way forward was to wring something positive out of every new day and to find an upside in every run, much like everyday runners. There were also times when I reconnected with that community in a way that reminded me why I appreciated the act of running, as opposed to competing. Kate Gustafson, a Canadian I'd met while training in Kenya, reached out and said she was headed to a running retreat in Tempe. She and I shared a passion for travel, and we always tried to get together when we randomly found ourselves in the same place. We picked up the conversation without missing a beat, as usual. She and her group of friends weren't professional runners, but their passion for the sport was contagious, and the dust they kicked up in Phoenix reeled me back to my time in Iten. They were dedicating themselves to strive for personal bests without the tangible goal of a major title or commercial benefit. It was a good shake-up for my perspective. Running wasn't just about comparison to others. It was internal: me versus me, a continual self-measurement I relished. I kept coming back to an idea I remembered from multiple readings of the Hindu scripture Bhagavad Gita:

Having passion for work alone might be the ultimate goal of all, because the work is the only thing that is

really, truly yours. You're entitled only to your labor.
You're not entitled to the fruit of your labor. The uni-
verse guarantees no results.

I stopped forcing myself toward a deliberate state of
cumulative fatigue and made a conscious decision to let
my body decide what I needed, rather than setting weekly
mileage targets. I asked myself what value a run would
bring to my training and ended up shedding a lot of junk
miles. Typically, on an easy day, I would have done 14 miles
in the morning and another 4 in the afternoon. When I felt
that an afternoon run would benefit me, I added it, but
more often found myself paring down to a single workout of
12 to 14 miles. I still averaged 105 to 110 miles a week during that block, with long runs of 16 or 18 miles. Those totals
weren't wildly different from what I'd done in previous
years, but I was letting intuition, not numbers, dictate the
schedule.

I knew my good days weren't making the world turn, but
I did have the sense I was in sync with the world as it turned,
using gravitational pull instead of letting it use me, moving
with a sense of purpose. It felt like this was what I was a
hundred percent built, wired, and designed to be doing—
not forever, but there and then. The work was more than
enough in those moments. The work was a bowl full of ripe
fruit.

◆ ◆ ◆

As far as the world was concerned, I was the athlete I'd always been. Only a handful of people had a clue what I'd been through and how it had changed me and the way I wanted to go about my job. I was about to test myself on a big stage in New York City and then a bigger one in Boston. The scale of those events made potential failure seem huge. I felt exposed and vulnerable in a way that scared me. I knew I wouldn't be ready or prepared to race in the way I was accustomed. Yet the point was still to find out how good I could be in the moment, even though my limits and my goals had shifted. Was I brave enough to take that on? I needed the kind of courage Atticus Finch spoke of in *To Kill a Mockingbird:* "It's when you know you're licked before you begin, but you begin anyway, and you see it through no matter what. You rarely win, but sometimes you do."

It was exhausting to think that big all the time, and I put aside those musings while I was running. That was sacred time to let my body do the talking, and tune in to my breathing and my surroundings. I seldom listened to music on a run. I didn't want to be distracted. If pain and boredom seeped in, I welcomed them. I had to be comfortable with that stress in a race situation.

When I wasn't running, I had music on almost constantly, and Macklemore was a fixture on my playlists. His first solo album in twelve years had come out a few months before. It had the feel of a comeback, even though he hadn't gone away—and I related to that.

> *You know I'm back like I never left*
> *Another sprint, another step*
> *Another day, another breath*
> *Been chasing dreams, but I never slept . . .*

> *I feel glorious, glorious*
> *Got a chance to start again*
> *I was born for this, born for this*
> *It's who I am, how could I forget?*
> *"Glorious" (2017)*

EVERY RUN WASN'T a shining rebirth, by any means. There was more than one day that February where I needed to leave a workout behind, and settled onto the couch in Reid's apartment to watch the PyeongChang Winter Games. It helped to follow athletes whose shoes I could walk in, even though they competed on snow and ice, and I was toiling in the desert. I was intimately familiar with the pressure athletes pile onto themselves, and feel from the world, for that once-every-four-years event—no matter what else they've accomplished.

If you want to learn a thing or two about handling failure, turn on the #Olympics. You'd be hard-pressed to find people who have failed more, but the greats keep showing up. It takes 10 years, and countless setbacks, to become an overnight success.

#TeamUSA #PyeongChang2018

—Twitter via @des_linden, 2/21/18

I FOUND MYSELF glued to the Alpine ski races, rooting for Lindsey Vonn. The advance hype was all about how this was probably her last shot to win an Olympic medal. I knew the outlines of Vonn's story—the times she'd picked herself up from wrecks that didn't look survivable, the catastrophic injury that had knocked her out of the last Winter Games. There were the standard poignant video clips comparing her to her younger self and the observation that, if she made the podium at age thirty-three, she would be the oldest female Alpine medalist in history. Eight years had passed since she'd won a gold medal at the 2010 Vancouver Games. Since then, her resilience and sustained excellence had put her on the brink of becoming the all-time FIS Alpine Ski World Cup wins leader. I was drawn to Vonn's perseverance. She wasn't going to accept being labeled as washed up or the idea that she should worry about her "legacy," a word I detested. She was going to take her swing. The fuck-you of it all appealed to me, and that wasn't hard to analyze. I felt as if I might be out of time and out of chances, yet here I was, still at it.

Seeing Vonn push off from the start house filled me with admiration. She was an aging athlete with far less racing ahead of her than behind, and absolutely nothing to prove. She was still competing at the highest level, but there was already endless talk about her and her heir apparent, Mikaela Shiffrin, a supremely gifted younger skier poised to supplant her in the public eye. Yet Vonn, with her reknit bones and repaired ligaments and the knowledge that any result short of winning would be second-guessed, was choosing to hurtle downhill at eighty miles per hour. Why?

The relevant and far better question in my mind was, *Why the hell not?*

And then Vonn crushed the course and wound up with the bronze medal. It was obvious she would have preferred to win, and I understood that only too well, but standing on that podium was a reward for self-determination. I felt my old outsider's defiance percolating. Sure, I had signed on to perform in front of the public a few times a year, and I accepted all the scrutiny and judgment that entailed. But I did my real job in private. I earned my agency as an athlete daily, just like Vonn, even though she was a megastar, and I had yet to achieve my A-goal. No one else was going to tell me when I was done. No one was going to tell me I was out of chances, or that I had no shot at improvement, or that it was someone else's turn.

Maybe tomorrow would be better. And if not, maybe the next day. I'd never know if I didn't get out the door and give myself a chance—advice I'd once resisted from my dad but secretly retained and now fully applied. *Right foot, left foot, repeat.* A mantra was taking shape in my head, although I didn't think of it that way initially, and I didn't take a lot of time to compose what I posted in early March, seven weeks before Boston:

> Some days it just flows, and I feel like I'm born to do this, other days it feels like I'm trudging through hell. Every day I make the choice to show up and see what I've got, and to try and be better. My advice: keep showing up.
>   #MondayMotivation #TogetherForward
>   —Twitter via @des_linden, 3/15/18

◆ ◆ ◆

THE NYC HALF had become important for me as a prelude to Boston in the last few years, but not because I wanted to shoot for a personal best or win it. It came at an ideal time, a month out, when I still had building to do before starting my taper. I treated it as an indicator workout, which is a lot easier to do in an elite field under competitive conditions

than a long training run on an average weekend. The half
offered a good environment to test out new uniforms, shoes,
and race-day nutrition, to scrape off the rust and shake out
the nerves. My usual goal was to run marathon pace on
dead legs, simulating the stress I'd experience in the last six
miles.

My self-imposed stakes were higher this time. I took the
inspiration I'd derived from Vonn's Olympic performance—
Why couldn't that be me?—and resolved to carry it forward.
I hoped for the kind of day I'd had episodically in Arizona,
where the best current version of myself emerged. New York
would be an interim yet true measure of my form instead of
a box to check off during my training block. I also understood the flip side. If I ran 1:18 or 1:20 instead of 1:12 or 1:13,
it would have implications for the near future. Athletes
come to major marathons dinged up all the time, but I was
sensitive to the fact that, starting with the July 2017 half in
Australia, I'd had almost a year of less than stellar racing,
including an unusual break in the fall. I wouldn't be able to
justify pretending that things were okay and taking a shot.
I'd have to pull the plug on Boston.

The first thing I had to do when I arrived in New York
was fulfill advance promotional obligations for Boston—
routine duty, but my uncertainty and stress about the up-
coming race made the ritual miserable. I felt like a fraud
sitting for an hour of filming, thinking, *I could actually*

have to pull out in a few days, while MK and the John Hancock marketing team were trying to drag some personality out of me for their social media clips, urging "More energy!" "More excitement!" Josh, MK, and I would normally spend time afterward catching up and making plans to hang out later, but I was uninterested in being social, and bolted.

EARLY ON DURING that build, John Hancock asked a few runners in the elite field to share their Spotify playlists. It was amusing to scroll through them and see how they reflected people's personalities. Anyone who paid attention to mine might have wondered about my frame of mind. I led off with Sturgill Simpson's "Living the Dream":

> *Ain't no point getting outta bed when you ain't living the dream*
> *It's like making a big old pot of coffee when you ain't got no cream*

Continued with Okkervil River's "For Real":

> *It's just a drive into the dark stretch,*
> *long stretch of night,*
> *really stretch this shaking mind.*

And finished up with Lana Del Rey's "Summertime Sadness," with a fair number of brooding, desolate songs in between. It was one big downer of a soundtrack and accurate for where I was a lot of the time.

Still, I felt a fair degree of optimism on a frigid race morning as we lined up in Brooklyn's Prospect Park, the new start for a significantly hillier, more challenging course the organization was debuting that year. Headwinds made for a forgiving early pace, a huge advantage for me, and my confidence grew as the race progressed.

How do I feel? Pretty good.

Midway through, with the pack still lagging, I chose to go to the front and try to break things open with an appropriate effort. I wound up finishing eighth in 1:13:33—slow by objective standards, but the time didn't matter. I'd competed well, a small reward for my months of work, and justified the decision to continue on the path to Boston.

Josh and I wandered Manhattan afterward until we found a place to celebrate with Bloody Marys. Our mood was somewhere between cautiously encouraged and ecstatic as we raised our glasses. I'd been on the quality end of my current form and gotten glimpses of my former self. What had seemed daunting before the race—pushing the pace, finding the drive to break and beat athletes, and reveling in the thrill of performing at the center of the running universe—now felt motivating again.

I knew I needed to consider how pushing myself too much in Boston could affect my long-term health. Hard as it was to accept, I might have to view 2018 as a stepping-stone, a means to a more distant but still attainable end. Yet my prospects, uncertain as they were, still felt more promising than they did in the days leading up to the Olympic marathon in London, when I had resigned myself to a DNF even as I packed ibuprofen in my gear bag.

I allowed myself to drift toward *Maybe I can.*

◆ ◆ ◆

THOSE FEW MILES when I pushed into the wind with nothing but road in front of me in New York gave me reassurance, and a revelation I hadn't necessarily expected.

I had spent a lot of time resisting the notion of being "just" a runner—especially being a long-distance runner. In college, I wanted to be a 1,500-meter runner, when it was obvious that I was better suited to the 5,000-meter or the 10,000-meter events. When I joined the Hansons, I was dead set on sticking with the 10,000 and never running a marathon. After years of trying to learn how to get out of my own way, I had finally figured out I needed to stay open to opportunity even when I couldn't create a positive outcome in my mind's eye—or even imagine myself enjoying the process. If running was what I did, not who I was, it was up to me to decide how long running would be central to my life, and set the terms. *You don't get what you deserve, you get what you negotiate.*

I WAS DOING what I once doubted was possible: creating the lifestyle I wanted as a runner, with plenty of room for the passions I'd made a point of cultivating over the last few years. Travel, reading, music, taking the dogs to the beach, refining my tastes in coffee and bourbon—I wasn't anywhere near willing to give them up. If running evaporated tomorrow, they would help give me my footing. The fierceness I felt about it took me back to a passage I had mentally underlined in a book by Thomas Friedman, *The Lexus and the Olive Tree: Understanding Globalization*: "Few things are more enraging to people than to have their identity or their sense of home stripped away. They will die for it, kill for it, sing for it, write poetry for it, and novelize about it. Because without a sense of home and belonging, life becomes barren and rootless. And life as a tumbleweed is no life at all."

Now, even during the most disorienting stretch of my life, when I was still trying to figure out if I had the will to rebuild, I had found new ways to redefine and embrace "the grind." Tapping into hope after setbacks, engineering solutions to obstacles, knowing there was more than one route that could lead me to that elusive state of flow—this was what grounded me and kept me from being buffeted by the fickle wind. That secret had been hiding in plain sight all along: I was most at home and in my element when I realized how much I still didn't know and immersed myself in learning.

Suddenly I wanted more than anything to be a runner at least for a little while longer. I was ready to scrap for that identity instead of fighting it. I would choose when to give it up. Until then, I was going to make the rest of the pack rip it out of my cold, dead hands.

◆ ◆ ◆

I WAS IN a rejuvenated frame of mind when I went to Boston after the New York City Half Marathon to do some more promotion and to log a twenty-miler, my longest run of the build, on the marathon course. Snow lingered by the side of the road in some places, but it was a gorgeous day, and I ran in shorts and short sleeves. MK drove ahead of me, stopping periodically to film and hand me fluids. I had initially confided bits and pieces about my health issues to her, but definitely underplayed them and hadn't given her any details about the setbacks and inconsistency of the last few months. "You look really good," she said. "You haven't looked like this in a long time. You look so smooth." I knew she meant it.

THE FIRST THING I always noticed when I did a Boston course tour was the quiet as I passed each 5k marker, where the crowds would stack several rows deep on race day. I heard nothing but wind in the stretch of woods near the Wellesley campus that would be transformed into a deafening corridor of sound. It was always good to conjure up the excitement of the event. I reabsorbed the undulations of the course, feeling the true start of the Newton hills before the right-hand turn at the fire station and the sting in my quads on the steepest drop of the course in Newton Lower Falls. I embraced the solitude of the early miles that allowed my mind to wander. After Mile 17, I began to see people training on the paved carriage path that parallels the road in the hills, but I stuck with the actual course, since the point was to reacquaint myself with it. Once I came off Heartbreak, I had to be more aware of dodging city traffic and pedestrians, and occasionally hopped onto the sidewalk in front of shops.

The downhills generated natural pace, making it easy to slip into my ingrained practice of visualization. I left doubt behind and began picturing myself making and covering moves and fighting for the win. *Hell no, I'm not done.* The irresistible, contagious magic of the city and the course pulled me into that reverie, the one where I always finished as the Boston Marathon champion.

There was a freshness in my stride that morning. The sensation of normalcy I'd felt in New York stayed with me, like a low and steady pilot light. I was running my favorite roads in the world, with blue skies and perfect temperatures and my good friend MK offering encouraging words. I was present and open to the hope and inspiration of the moment. It was the kind of day I lived for, even though there was no guarantee I could repeat it the next day—or on race day.

MILE 20

W E'RE IN THE Newton hills now, the toughest part of the course. I'm solo, chasing.

The rain hasn't let up. It's coming down in sheets. And Chesir hasn't pulled away. Even with the low visibility, I'm close enough to her—and to the leader, Daska—to see the press trucks up ahead, with waterlogged camera crews and reporters facing us, standing backward on the truck beds.

If I can see them, they can definitely see me.

As we near the crest of Heartbreak Hill, I'm in frame and finally engaged in the race that means so much to me. I've fully ditched the idea of abandoning. There's no way, not if I'm physically capable of getting to the end.

When we come over the top, I'm finally within reach of Chesir, who has closed the gap on Daska. Chesir has been the sacrificial lamb, too naive to know she's done too much work, too inexperienced to realize how much you gain by running the tangents correctly. She's missed every single one. I'm a savvy vet on this course and have been running them to perfection, slicing down on Chesir simply by running the most efficient path.

She keeps pressing to catch Daska—too quickly, in my mind, expending precious energy and seemingly unaware that it would be to her advantage if we split the work. I'm not about to complain. Chesir is towing me up to Daska, and if we're able to catch her, she'll be done. I allow myself to think about coasting the rest of the way, avoiding any more risk, and finishing second. That would be a massive, unthinkable victory compared with where I started this morning.

Runner-up in Boston. Been there.

Coming up two seconds short in 2011 left a burn that has never fully healed.

My mind rebels.

Chesir blows by Daska as the pair crest Heartbreak Hill, just before Mile 21. In a mere fifteen seconds, I'm on Chesir's heels. It's decision time. I can either sit behind her or test her.

I don't hesitate. I pass her with an authority I couldn't have summoned a few months before—or even the previous night, when I pondered whether I was capable of being competitive on this day and what it could cost me to try. Then I elect to skip the next fluid station to accelerate fully and try to create some separation.

How will she respond? Or will she?

Nothing is the same as it was in 2011, except the mental blueprint I know I have to follow from here on. The race resets when we come off Heartbreak. It's time to turn the screws and put away the chasers. I need to grind down the competition for the next four miles all the way to Boylston Street. As I know well from past history, once the leader is out of sight, it becomes increasingly hard to forge on with any semblance of hope. The natural inclination is to start worrying about who's on your heels and how to preserve what you have.

I head down the steep downhill past the Chestnut Hill Reservoir. It's hard to hear through the downpour and my saturated headband, but it's possible there's a gap.

The pace has been slowing, but the effort still feels right. The last few months have taught me to value effort over pace, by necessity.

I've scraped the bottom of a well of fatigue over this last year, not once but many times, feeling significantly worse than the way I feel in this moment. I've been baffled by why I couldn't make more linear progress, why my training was so maddeningly erratic when consistency was my core identity—a word that cropped up in practically every story written about me. I've run miles at an eight-minute pace that feel like full-on sprints. I've been winded from climbing a single flight of stairs, muscles burning the way they did in the last two hundred meters in 2011. I've been slowly clawing my way back to the point where I could get through enough of the race to be able to bail without betraying just how deep a hole I'd been in.

Yet some days I'd head out and be my normal self—or, maybe more properly, my former self—and roll through a tempo: 5:25, click; 5:25, click; 5:25, click. Effortless, as if I was born for it.

Other days, for no discernible reason, I'd push harder and lose ground, slower by a minute or more: 6:25, 6:43, 6:50. The definition of diminishing returns. I'd contemplate cutting the run short, but then force myself to finish the work anyway, telling myself those numbers were what a hard effort amounted to on that day. That was what I had come to think of as accomplishment—a tough sell after judging my self-worth by the stopwatch for twenty years, but I made the shift.

Now, leading the Boston Marathon with four miles to go—a position my mind barely accepts as real—I apply that learning. I plug away at what I feel like is my maximum effort on this day, in these conditions, in this moment.

The course is obdurate. The course doesn't know I'm running in historically bad conditions, that every step is another incremental gamble with my body, that a lifelong goal suddenly feels tangible to me under the most unlikely circumstances possible.

With my glycogen reserves nearly gone, these last few miles become a battle of will. It's the challenge I fell in love with. Josh always says you run the first 20 miles with your head and the last 6.2 with your heart, and the back end of Boston is unlike any other marathon. The steep descents down Chestnut Hill, through Brookline, and into the city should help me speed home, unless I've been too aggressive early; this race exposes early mistakes like no other, and I've made a few. Downhills on battered quads become a painful disaster, and runners who'd been impatient early on always suffer here, slowing to a crawl over the final few miles. The biggest variable now isn't just Chesir, or any chasers behind her. It's the uncertainty that confronts anyone in my position: How will I respond when things get tough?

LOYALTY SHOWS UP

FOUR DAYS BEFORE the marathon, I set my watch, stepped out of our front door in Rochester, and began to run. Gravel crunched underfoot, then gave way to paved road. I headed for the familiar loop around Stony Creek Lake. It was fifty-four degrees, partly cloudy, with light winds out of the south—typical early-April weather.

My plan was to do two miles at marathon pace, followed by 4 × 800 meters faster than marathon pace, followed by another two miles at ten seconds faster than marathon pace. The progression would let me build into the workout and test both turnover and strength. It was a more aggressive session than I would have attempted at this point in past years. Part of me was already looking beyond race day and the prospect that I wouldn't finish. I might run a half marathon later in the spring or summer; I was essentially training through Boston. I had felt pretty lackluster in the weeks since the New

York Half. The Boston course tour had been an exception, but not the kind of hard workout that left me thinking, *I'm super fit*. I wanted to push myself and see what happened.

The racing flats I wore were painted black from the uppers to the soles, obscuring the logos. They'd been hand delivered to me a couple of days before by Bryan Bhark, representing the Brooks Footwear Team that had been hammering away to finish them. He'd apologized as he pulled them out of his backpack in a Traverse City coffee shop. I'd put them on and taken a few strides in the street as he watched. Getting brand-new flats this close to a major race was almost unheard of. There would be no time for feedback or adjustments if I had issues with them, no avoiding the unexpected—unfamiliar stress on my body, or chafing and blisters in places where I didn't have protective calluses. Bryan had flown in from Seattle so he could talk to me face-to-face; another member of the Footwear Team, Nikhil Jain, was doing the same with my teammate Shadrack Biwott in Florida. They told us they hoped we'd wear the shoes in Boston, but would understand if we opted not to.

Brooks had been the first company to commit to chasing Nike's state-of-the-art shoe technology, and this was the first version of the flats intended to close the performance gap. The shoes had been shaped with Dathan Ritzenhein's input when he joined the Hansons' group after his last Nike contract had expired. Dathan had made it known that he preferred a stiffer shoe, and he'd been training and racing in the prototypes for a few months now, preparing for the first major with his new team.

As Bryan and I talked, a Twitter alert lit up my phone: An injury had forced Dathan to withdraw from the Boston Marathon. The irony was thick. He'd been at the head of the line for the new flats, while other runners in the Hansons' group without his pull—including me—had to hound the company about the competitive importance of getting them. That was an involved and expensive process; we were light-years from the time when Nike cofounder Bill Bowerman used a waffle iron to create an early model, and shoe molds alone cost an average of $50,000 per size run. Brooks ultimately had agreed to make shoes for Shadrack and me in time for Boston.

The shoes were emblematic of the bigger questions I was grappling with. I didn't want to feel defeated before I even started. And if I somehow was able to finish, I'd be drawing on a deep, visceral reserve that wasn't just about the accumulated miles in my legs. It was about the people and experiences that had sustained me through all those miles. That's what I tapped into at the end of marathons, and it required a clear head even as my tired legs churned on. *You run the last 6.2 with your heart.* I couldn't afford to be distracted by some issue with my feet.

My six-mile workout, the last real run I'd do ahead of Boston, was about self-observation rather than emotion. I tried to concentrate on the actual sensation of the flats, not the concept. My first impressions weren't good; the shoes struck me as heavy and overly rigid. The traction was decent, but the one-inch-wide split in the sole, meant to show off the carbon plate, tended to pick up rocks that size or larger. My discomfort smoothed out as I accelerated my pace in the middle of the workout. The flats began to feel less cumbersome and more responsive, with good pop. I allowed myself to be pleasantly surprised. I was also aware that energy might shift again and again over a longer distance. I finished the run feeling both strong and ambivalent. Did the shoes seem better because I had a good workout, or did I have a better workout because of the shoes? Did that matter? Should I race in them or default to a sure thing? I added that to the long list of choices I had to make.

Ryan and I took off for Boston that afternoon, a wheels-up I normally relished. I didn't have quite the same level of dread I'd felt before London 2012, but I was used to having a consistent body of work under my belt and a firm grasp on my fitness, and I wasn't there. Despite the hints of optimism I'd experienced over the past few months, hard realism had left me without the usual nervous energy I felt at this point, the constructive anxiety of knowing this year could be my year.

◆ ◆ ◆

FRIDAY THE 13TH. The first item on my wall-to-wall prerace schedule: the ritual of the elite athlete media conference in the Fairmont Copley ballroom. It was the same high-decibel, organized chaos every year. A dozen runners sat at tables a few feet apart as reporters moved from station to station, clustering around with notebooks, cameras, digital recorders, and smartphones. When I took my place under the glittering chandeliers, I had never been more ready for one specific question in my life. A real answer might cost me my job, but I still felt as if someone *should* ask it. I didn't have a prepared answer—I just knew I would be straightforward. I also knew how my answer would land, and I was ready for that, too. I was living in the land of zero fucks given.

Reporters circulated between the top American athletes—Shalane and me, along with Jordan Hasay and Molly Huddle, making her Boston debut. Yes, I'd skipped a fall marathon. Yes, it would have been best to have had a more consistent year since the last time I'd sat in this room, but I was hoping the tweaks I'd made in training would set me up for the future. As I heard myself talk, I felt the lure of magical thinking: If I said things, I could make them happen. *My form looked fine in New York. If I say it's fine, maybe it will be fine.*

I had started to wonder if I might be off the hook when Jonathan Gault, from the running website LetsRun.com, walked over with his video cam poised. Almost five minutes into the interview, he said, "So, I'm curious . . ."

I braced for the question I had been anticipating for months, the one that had prompted me to voice my concerns to Brooks, the inevitable consequence of adding

Dathan to the team while the Nike Oregon Project was still
under active investigation by the US Anti-Doping Agency.
Up to now, I'd been fine staying in my lane and focusing on
myself. I knew my answer would put an end to that superfi-
cial coexistence.

Jonathan asked how I felt about the Hansons signing
Dathan.

"What were your thoughts on that? Do you support
that?"

I kept my gaze steady. I shook my head. I couldn't help a
small, tense half laugh.

"No. Not especially . . . But my name's not on the jersey.
We can talk team, team, team, but, ultimately, two guys
make the decision. So, it's not really my call. Hopefully it all
works out and no lines were crossed, but until that's kind of
cleared, I can't be super-supportive.

"It puts me in a tough spot. It's hard to be vocal about
anti-doping when someone can say, 'What about you? What
about this?'"

As resolved as I had been beforehand, and as strong and
composed as I tried to sound, in real time I was fighting to
control panic. I was short of breath, my heart was racing,
and I felt as if my chest and throat were closing up.

Those few minutes felt both inevitable and drastic. I had
deliberately dodged having this very conversation with the
Hansons. I knew it would permanently rupture a once-

positive relationship that had been pivotal in my development as an athlete and had landed me in a place that became my home. I had played it out in my head many times: I'd ask them to explain how they justified signing Dathan, they would justify it, and I would find that untenable. As long as we didn't actually have the conversation, there would be no formal parting of the ways, just a continued slow fraying from distance and avoidance. I still felt gratitude and appreciation toward the brothers, and in one idealistic corner of my mind, I hoped we could salvage a friendship. But I knew we would never see eye to eye on this, and it would force some big decisions—including, perhaps, about my future with Brooks.

Josh had several clients in the room, and I went over to him as people began to file out. My facial expression probably said it all: *This just happened.* I gave him a brief synopsis anyway as we walked to my next obligation, a video sit-down for NBC. He was supportive and completely unsurprised. I had been direct with him on where I stood and clear about the fact that I wouldn't sugarcoat my answer if I was asked about it. Josh had never discouraged me from being honest, but he was always candid about the ripple effect honesty could have, and we both knew it wouldn't take long for these particular ripples to start spreading.

I couldn't have been more tense and distracted, but I also had to stick to my itinerary. Next up was a Brooks promotional event where I rode the T to a photo signing at a downtown shoe store while a bunch of community runners covered the same distance, trying to "beat" me. Josh and I got there almost simultaneously with Kevin, and the three of us spent ten awkward minutes sitting outside on the curb, waiting for the event to start. Once we were inside, time crawled by. Josh monitored his phone. When social media began lighting up with the LetsRun.com video, we bowed out. I left convinced that Kevin and Keith would be actively rooting against me come Monday or, at the very least, would be unperturbed if I looked awful and couldn't finish, despite the fact that I was still wearing their jersey.

Dathan was a golden boy of American distance running, the ultimate insider. Whatever opinions people harbored about Salazar or the Hansons, I had broken ranks as far as the industry was concerned, and I knew my comments would rile up the good old boys in the running world. People wanted "clean sport" but didn't like hearing hard truths. I could feel their collective eyes on me that night at the formal dinner hosted by John Hancock, but no one had the balls to actually confront me. A handful of younger runners approached me privately and thanked me for expressing what they didn't think they had standing to say.

Brooks had its own press conference scheduled at the Seaport Hotel the next day. It was a familiar drill: an athlete panel followed by individual breakdown sessions where I'd be alone at a table with reporters. I was asked to arrive early to get talking points on how I would handle potential questions about the Hansons and Dathan. It turned into a bit of a scolding, ironically, since I had foreseen this exact scenario and asked to have this conversation months ago. I'm sure my body language read *I told you so.*

I worked at smiling, avoiding clichés, and trying to temper expectations. It was beautiful in Boston that day, but the forecast was looking ominous, or so I'd heard—past experience told me it would change multiple times, and I never checked the weather before forty-eight hours out. Having run Boston in every condition, I had answers ready and went on autopilot.

"It's going to run like a thirty-miler."

"Mistakes in Boston always cost you in the later miles, but mistakes in these conditions will be highlighted with an exclamation point."

"Smart runners will be rewarded."

The press conference itself wound up being anticlimactic. Nobody dug into Dathan or anything else controversial. My fight-or-flight adrenaline ebbed away. My emotional reserves were on empty. I told myself I needed to be rational about any backlash. It was just one more discomfort to manage.

Neither Josh nor I said a word on the fifteen-minute cab ride back to the Fairmont. I didn't break the silence until we were alone in the hotel elevator, when I told him I didn't see myself doing any more meaningful races. "I'm so over this,"

I said. "I'm running Turkey Trots and Jingle Jogs until my contract is up. None of this is fun anymore."

◆ ◆ ◆

JOHN BALL WAS a predictably calming presence that weekend. As he put me through one last prerace round of stretches and massage, he continued to counsel that it might be unwise for my long-term health to go all out or even try to finish.

"Nothing about the way you guys train is normal or especially healthy," he said. "This is going to buy you time to keep building back slowly instead of just hammering yourself right back into the well. Everyone is going to think you had a bad one because of the unnecessary stress of the press conference."

By "everyone," John meant the people who counted in my business life: sponsors and event organizers. There was an easy explanation for my only previous DNF—a cracked femur—but I had no experience with what could happen after a less obvious letdown, and the impact it might have on invitations or appearance fees. I considered preempting any postrace questions by saying I'd had food poisoning the day before, or rolled an ankle, or something else that hurt my form temporarily.

It didn't feel great to premeditate excuses for a race that

meant so much to me—a scant year after I had every hope of winning it. Yet as unsettling as it was to think that way, I appreciated John's logic and his deep understanding of how I was built psychologically. Here was a friend and adviser who normally prepped me to win; now he was pivoting to help me manage running with restraint and limited expectations. It was a pragmatic way to frame ambition, consistent with John's style, which was to give me difficult feedback in a compassionate manner.

I wanted to believe his view that this would be a steppingstone back to full health, but I couldn't shake the thought that I was running out of road. There were three years left on my Brooks contract, and I had to live up to the terms, but in that moment, it felt more like a forced march than a dream job. I was exhausted on so many levels and couldn't see mustering the fight to improve and continue to chase great performances.

Yet I was discounting something in that moment. Maybe a lot of things. Mostly, the space between my ears, where I had built up a different kind of endurance. I couldn't rip out a lifetime of competitive wiring overnight. And I had just finished the strangest, possibly most instructive training block of my life, where I'd managed to find something to gain from every workout.

I had spent so many hours, weeks, and months visualizing success on this course that I found it almost impossible to picture the act of slowing down and stepping off. Instead, my thoughts skipped ahead to the people who would be waiting for me afterward. Natalie was already in Boston; that was never in question. She had cheered at my marathon debut, comforted me after the gut-wrenching 2008 Olympic trials, gone nuts during my 2011 stretch duel, and immediately understood all the good that would come of that finish. As usual, she was following a path I admired, pursuing what made her happy and being unwilling to settle for less. She'd completely switched careers, deciding to become a family therapist, and was working her way through grad school. She had reconnected with Brad Steele, a friend from our childhood, and I could tell this relationship might be headed for something lasting. Yet no matter what Natalie had going in her own life, she always made time to be at my biggest races. She would be there, she would say exactly the right thing, and I would hear it. The image steadied me.

◆ ◆ ◆

It snowed Sunday morning, killing my incentive to leave the hotel for a shakeout run. I bunkered in and relaxed, trying to stick to my normal day-before routine. Late in the day, it occurred to me that I hadn't eaten much all weekend. *What if I decide to finish? No matter how far I'm going to run, I have to be prepared.* I walked to the hospitality room and filled a to-go box with traditional prerace carbs: pasta and Bolognese sauce, plain rice.

Back in my room, I began working through my night-before checklist, pinning my race bib to my jersey, filling bottles with electrolyte-carb mix. They were labeled with my name and color coded in order of the tables where race volunteers would place them. Two had caffeine, the rest didn't, but I found myself losing track of which was which. I was usually on top of those details, but shrugged it off. It probably wouldn't matter.

In the middle of my haphazard organizing, an update popped on my phone: Jordan Hasay had scratched from the race with a heel injury. It didn't surprise me, other than the fact that she'd waited so long. She'd been all smiles at the press conference, but she'd been overheard afterward talking about having an MRI, and rumors that she was hurt had been circulating for about a month. Ryan walked in as I was reading the news. He and I agreed that it wouldn't make much difference in my plan or anyone else's. There had been a lot of buzz about seeing her line up against Molly and Shalane for the first time, and she would have had a good shot to finish as top American, but she also wasn't one to dictate tactics.

Ryan brought up the miserable weather slamming the city. I hadn't been outside all day, so I did a double take when I checked the hourly forecast: temperatures in the high thirties at the start, relentless heavy rain, and winds of fifteen to twenty-five miles per hour, gusting to forty-five. Insane. And good cover for me if I dropped out before the finish. I wouldn't be alone.

Reid was in town—he'd run the BAA 5K a couple of days before—and stopped by with his girlfriend, Sarah Pagano, to wish me good luck. We were chatting idly when Josh arrived, clearly in a great mood. I knew he'd just had a meeting with the Brooks Sports Marketing team. Subject: my career.

I kept my tone casual. "Am I fired? Am I still wearing their stuff Tuesday—or even tomorrow?"

"No. It's all good," Josh said. "I think everything's going to be fine. They're rolling out potential plans for the next couple of years. We'll figure it out. Let's just get through tomorrow, and we can talk about what the rest of it looks like down the line, later."

The company reps had said they would sort out my place with or without the Hansons, something we hadn't been certain of a day before. Relief washed over me, and good energy filled the room. It suddenly felt like a normal race eve, chatting comfortably with my buddies.

At about nine o'clock, Josh got up to go. "Get some sleep," he said, knowing I probably wouldn't. The door shut behind him, leaving Ryan and me alone.

"You have a shot," Ryan said. "Everything's really good for you. You're in a great spot with this news from Josh.

You'll be okay. You're still going to have a contract, you're not going to have to worry about that. So just try."

I looked at him. At first it sounded like he just wanted to build on the positive vibe of the last hour. Then I realized he was talking specifically about the race. Conditions were perfect for me, he was saying, not just as an alibi but as a true competitive edge.

"Everybody is going to freak out, and you know how to run in this garbage," Ryan said. "You've done enough workouts during the buildup to be competitive. Just try, and see what happens. If you have to drop out, fine, but don't head to the line planning on dropping out. You're mentally tougher than everyone. This is perfect for you."

My first reaction was mild resistance.

"I need to talk to John," I said. "I'll talk to John tomorrow, but I don't want to lose sight of the fact that the whole point of this was not setting myself back for another year.

"We can't get caught up in this emotional moment and then just throw out what John and I have been talking about for months. The bigger goal doesn't just change because we're in a good mood or because the weather's bad. You can't just throw out everything that was logical just because right now it feels like it might be a good idea."

Ryan was undeterred. "I've seen the last three weeks of work. They're not perfect, but I know you've done enough.

You're more prepared than you're giving yourself credit for. Don't count yourself out."

His tone took on a rare urgency: half pleading, half exasperated.

"You have to try."

His unwavering confidence took me aback. And it moved me. Ryan and I had drawn a line between our personal and professional lives. We shared everything, but I trusted him to know what was best for his work, and he trusted me to decide what was best for mine. The fact that he'd spoken so strongly was unprecedented and gave me pause. There was no one more invested in my happiness and no one who saw me with such clarity.

Years before, Ryan had watched me argue fiercely with the Hansons about the idea of holding back at my Boston debut. That self-belief was part of what had drawn him to me. Now he was asking me to fight for myself, to be true to the core of that conviction, which was still intact. What if he was onto something?

"I totally understand where you're coming from," I said. "I actually do think this is really great. I wish I were in better shape. If it were a normal year, I'd be stoked. You're right, you're absolutely right, this is all really good stuff for me, but I want to make sure John's not like, 'That's the dumbest thing you could do right now.'"

My mind continued to wrestle with the events of the day

and the decisions I had to make as we headed for bed. This might be the last major race of my career. I could have deferred my entry for a year, but I hadn't. Even after John suggested I should consider dropping out because it might be the wisest thing for me, I'd kept doing the work as well as I could, thinking I might come around. And Ryan was aware of that. He'd just kept his thoughts to himself until now.

Why would it be wrong to try to finish? What did I have to lose? To gain? To learn? The last year had made me uncertain of many things, and I wasn't sure I was nimble enough to be present to possibility, to take this definitive of a turn in my thinking, to allow room for the worst day to become, potentially, a great day. I'd already cracked the door in my own mind. Now it was wedged open.

I had chosen to run. Ryan wanted me to gamble on my heart and choose to race.

◆ ◆ ◆

IT'S IMPOSSIBLE TO get quality sleep the night before a major marathon. Anyone who says differently is either a liar or a psychopath. I am neither, so I wasn't surprised to be awake at four-thirty after maybe six restless hours. I rolled out of bed, trying not to disturb Ryan, and headed blindly for the bathroom in the dark. The marble floor felt smooth and cool on my bare feet. I took a deep breath and savored the

clean, comforting smell of whatever posh toiletry product
they stocked at the Fairmont. This peaceful, meditative moment was the last bit of solitude I would have for many
hours. My next chance to be alone and process would be
when I stepped into the shower to wash away my effort and
results.

I always started Boston race day with the same question.
Will my life be any different the next time I stand here? That
possibility, the idea that I could leave this hotel room a runner and return a champion—knowing everything could
change based on what I did over the next several hours—
had always been motivating and exciting to me. I wanted to
tap into the energy I'd felt the night before, to allow myself
to be upbeat, but this wasn't like any other race day. I
dreaded the thought of being back in this spot, alone with
someone I disliked: a quitter.

Routine is everything, and I stuck to mine despite my
internal churning. I knew that when I emerged from the
bathroom in my race gear, my coffee and breakfast would
be waiting, and Ryan would be prepping a second coffee for
me to take on the fifty-minute bus ride to the start in Hopkinton. Sure enough, my fuel was ready: a bagel with peanut
butter, a bowl of white rice, and hot coffee, along with Ryan's ever-encouraging smile. Outwardly, he was his cheerful
morning self, pampering me like a princess, but he picked
at his eggs and bacon—a dead giveaway that he was

nervous. I resolved to stay even-keeled. The gun was still several hours away, and it was far too early to start trying to pump myself up to do what I needed to do.

We worked through our breakfast ritual until a quarter to six, when it was time to leave the comfort of the room. I grabbed my gear bag stuffed with two of everything, options to keep myself warm and dry—socks, gloves, jackets, head-bands, hats, racing flats—and took the elevator down to the ground floor, where we stepped into the palatial, blindingly bright expanse of the Fairmont lobby. Pendulous crystal chandeliers reflected off mirrored walls, gilt molding, and pristine white marble floors. The space was rapidly filling with lean figures in sweatsuits and neon running shoes. Running royalty, in all our finery.

This moment was always what made race day feel real for the first time, and, as usual, my nerves hit hard. I felt a brief rush of light-headedness and my stomach lurched as we moved through buzzing groups of agents, athletes, coaches, brand managers, family, and friends toward the ballroom doors. Only those with credentials were allowed to cross that threshold, so this was where I had to leave Ryan.

"You're going to be fine," he said. "You know what to do if it feels like it's falling apart out there, but don't give up before this thing even gets going. You're mentally stronger than anyone else. I know you'll make the right decisions."

He still wasn't willing to concede anything. *He's speaking from emotion, not logic,* I thought. I smiled and nodded. It wasn't worth parting on a bad note. We hugged, and he wished me luck.

MK greeted me at the athlete check-in table and made sure I had a uniform, my two bibs, and shoes. I gave her a hard time about treating me like a child. As she snapped a quick photo of me for Hancock's Twitter feed, my mind drifted to the trivial. *This image is bringing outsiders into one of the most important rooms in running, and I should have spent some time combing my hair. It looks like shit.*

Normally, I would have enjoyed the sight of MK's friendly face and our habitual banter, but on a deeper level, I knew this was the toughest interaction I would have all morning. Her invitation for this year had been such a crucial gesture. The mere act of lining up at the start without my usual competitive mindset and ambition meant that I was likely about to disappoint someone I owed so much, someone who had gone to bat for me time and again. The nerves that had been making my stomach crawl gave way to a sharper sensation, a sting of obligation and guilt. It felt exactly the way my hair looked: like shit.

◆ ◆ ◆

EVERY MARATHON MONDAY, the Fairmont ballroom is transformed into a greenroom where celebrities gather before the biggest show in running. I was among a crowd of Abbott World Marathon Majors champions, Olympic medalists, and former national and world record holders. It reminded me, as if I needed one more thing to feel insecure about, that my résumé lacked a real highlight, and there was no guarantee I'd do anything truly noteworthy in my career.

I crossed paths with Joan Benoit Samuelson, who took a second to wish me good luck.

"You are the master of these conditions," she said.

I joked that today I felt like another kind of Masters runner—an amateur in the forty-plus age group—but the wisecrack seemed to be lost on her. Most of the assembled cast have never really gotten anything about me. I would always feel like an outsider in this room and others like it, and that was fine. I had made my peace with it over the years. I walked to the back of the room, chose a seat away from the chaos, put my head back, closed my eyes, and tried to visualize the end of the day.

The chairs around me filled in slowly as athletes continued to arrive. Representatives from different brands stood near the check-in table, distributing last-minute product to their sponsored athletes. A Nike rep shoved brand-new windbreakers at all of his runners—a smart addition on a wet day. We got a short speech from John Hancock CEO Marianne Harrison, and then MK followed up with her standard quick pep talk.

"You are here because we believe in you," she said. "All of you have a chance to win this race."

If only I agreed with her.

"We are proud of each and every one of you. We're going to take one last photo of the full team, and then we will line up and head out to the buses. Good luck, everyone."

The athletes shuffled out. In the crowded lobby, family members, agents, and coaches waiting for one last peek had their phones held up, ready to shoot pictures and video; TV crews worked to grab footage of this moment, when the fastest distance runners in the world looked fresh and unscathed by effort. Their glaring lights were uncomfortably warm. Behind us, a transition began: staff started rolling in massage tables, coolers filled with recovery drinks, hot towels, blankets, and first aid equipment. We'd be back here, recovering, soon enough.

JUST BEFORE SIX-THIRTY, we lined up near two sets of heavy, brass-framed doors, the last barriers between us and the elements. Josh jumped in next to me and gave me a sympathetic smile as we pushed silently through the first set of doors. It's in every agent's interest to make sure his or her athletes are on time for the bus, but Josh was there for more than selfish reasons. He knew today could shape up to be one of the worst days of my career, and friendship would be the most important thing he could offer me. Loyalty shows up, even when it's inconvenient.

A John Hancock employee was handing out white towels marked with the signature logo—"Elite Athlete Team"— inside the olive wreath. I took two. As we passed through the second set of doors, a howling blast of frigid wind hit us like a physical blow. I could hear its forceful whistle even with my ears tucked under a winter hat. Stinging, freezing rain pelted our faces, sapping warmth from my lips and cheeks. It was the first time I'd left the hotel in more than twenty-four hours, and I hadn't quite registered the degree of awful during my quick skim of the forecast the night before. Clearly, the wind and rain would be with us all morning. Within two steps, my team towels were drenched, along with the rest of me. I glanced at Josh, who had one hand clamped on his Padres hat to keep the gusts from whipping it away, and the other hand shielding his eyes from the sideways rain.

I yelled over the wind, "Oh shit, so this is the weather everyone has been talking about!"

Josh yelled back, deadpan, "Yeah, I guess it's supposed to rain a little today!"

The absurdity of the situation was so obvious that we began laughing hysterically. Anyone watching us no doubt would have thought we were as insane as the weather. Our short walk down Trinity Place brought a minor epiphany:

Everyone was going to suffer today, but I would bet nobody had managed suffering the way I had over the previous eight months.

We ducked into the Clarendon Street garage where the VIP buses were lined up, then paused awkwardly and lingered. There were no perfect words for this moment, but Josh tried anyway.

"You've done everything you needed to do to make the best of this," he said. "We took care of the hardest part in New York, and I know I can take care of your future with Brooks beyond today."

I'd been fighting back tears for months in these talks with him. Just as I counted on seeing Natalie and Ryan after I finished, I could always depend on Josh to be there at dawn for the start, to make this walk with me. We had talked about this race for years, and we'd never stopped believing our shared vision and conviction that one of these days was going to be my day. Our bond was among the handful of relationships that meant I was never truly alone at the start line. I wanted to deliver for my husband, my sister, my parents, my physio, my industry mentor, and my agent, who had repped me in the true sense of the word, putting in the hours to make sure I got what I was worth. I hated thinking I wouldn't be able to pull my weight this time. My eyes welled up. Maybe he'd assume it was the rain.

"Thanks for working hard for me," I said. "I appreciate it. I'll see you soon."

He gave me a quick hug and said what I had come to expect from him but never took for granted.

"I'm proud of you no matter what happens out there."

MILE 26

Now that I have so much at stake, abruptly, I feel fear for the first time all day. My muscles go taut, and my heart rate rises, which actually isn't the worst sensation in my numb, half-frozen state. I have no idea where Chesir is, how close she is to me. I know I'm slowing, and she—or someone—must be narrowing the gap. Part of me is waiting for the dreaded, inevitable blowup, my body calling in its chips, the race reverting to form and me to my standard role of valiant supporting actress.

I'm still dialed in mentally. I know every landmark, sign, and pothole on this course, and I'm using them to stay focused and in the present.

The section of Beacon Street that takes us over the Mass Pike is a small but punchy incline that feels significant this late in the race. As I churn uphill, I take another risk by skipping yet another bottle, passing blurry but familiar faces working the elite athlete fluid tables.

The crowds are actually building, even in this weather, and I try to concentrate on the cheering. Gaps between cheers can be clues to where the next runner is. I strain to listen. Nothing. I think my drenched headband must be muffling sound, or that I'm so cold I've lost all ability to comprehend.

A 3-D version of this course lives permanently in my head, where I've run it countless times, incorporating the five I've raced before. I've never once imagined it quite like this.

I'm approaching the Massachusetts Avenue underpass, which means there's just under a mile to go. I know MK's family normally cheers from the lawn around this part of the course. I picture them watching from somewhere indoors, where it's warm.

Thinking of MK reminds me abruptly that I should peel off my jacket for the finishing photo so that the winning images will show my jersey and properly placed bib. I fiddle with the zipper in the few seconds I'm under the shelter of the bridge. No luck. My hands are frozen stiff. I tug with my teeth and then remember I'm still very much in a race, still being chased, and my vision is premature. I've lost this race by two seconds before, and I won't do even the smallest thing to jeopardize it this time. The jacket stays on.

Right on Hereford . . .

It feels like Mount Hereford at this point in the race. The incline isn't even perceptible on a casual walk, but at Mile 25, it's a leg burner.

One more turn before I'll be within sight of the most iconic finish line in all of marathoning, the one that mesmerized me and captured my heart in 2007, the one that had changed the course of my life from point-to-point into long loops, compelling me to return again and again and again. This time, there's no one between me and the tape.

I know in this moment that I can win. I've preserved my legs enough for one last fight. If someone is going to pass me when I take that last left, she's been working much harder than I have over the last several miles, not maintaining but chasing. In my heart, I think that's not possible. I've finally managed to outwork an entire elite field.

Left on Boylston . . .

I'm jolted by the strongest wind gusts and sideways rain I've faced all day—a bookend to the shock of exiting the double doors at the Fairmont that morning, and so loud that it rivals the wild, almost disbelieving roars of the crowd when I make the turn by myself. Boylston suddenly seems enormously wide to me, probably because I'm alone on the road, the center of attention. I'm inside a rarefied space, an outsider no more.

I let a smile creep halfway across my face. I can't help it. This is beyond absurd.

Let's fucking go.

I charge toward the right side of the road, the winner's lane, swiping water away from my eyes. I pass the Lenox Hotel, where my legs seized up on me in 2011, and think, *Damn, it's close to the finish line.* Race staff line the finish chute, waving me in. I hear the public address announcer's voice booming from the loudspeaker:

"And here comes your 2018 Boston Marathon champion, Desiree Linden."

◆   ◆   ◆

As SOON AS I break the tape, I instinctively bring my hands to my mouth in the universal human reaction to shock— and also because I desperately need to warm my frozen fingers. A small figure in a dark windbreaker is coming at me like an arrow. It's not until she's about to wrap her arms around me that I recognize the face shielded by the hood belongs to Joan Benoit Samuelson. It's really happening. I'm hugging the most legendary figure in American women's marathoning at this blue-and-gold finish line that now belongs to both of us. Joan repeats what she told me before the start, when I couldn't have hallucinated this scene: "I knew it was going to be your day. I said you are the master of these conditions."

My longtime friend Dean Mini, who manages race security, approaches me, his face glowing, and drapes an

American flag around my shoulders. Jack Fleming from the BAA—who treated me like I belonged at this race on my first tour of the offices so many years ago—steers me gently a few more steps away from the finish, where I'm enveloped by the only two people who can fully appreciate how unlikely this is.

Josh is crying. He has physically dragged Ryan out of the designated box where they had been told to wait and into the finish area. Thousands of people—millions more on TV—see the three of us clutch one another, but for those few seconds, we are by ourselves on Boylston Street. I finally manage to croak out something over the commotion: "I can't believe that just fucking happened." I look at Ryan, who is smiling his radiant smile, and I know that he can believe it and hadn't given up on me or that dream for a second.

This is my real finish line. I should have known I could run through anything to get here.

ANOTHER SEASON

I STEPPED ONTO THE podium, shivering sufficiently from cold and emotion that the blanket draped around my shoulders kept slipping off. I lowered my head for the gold-dipped olive wreath. It felt weightless, delicate, as if it might crumble any second. Then I hefted the sterling silver champions' trophy that was half my size, with blue and yellow streamers trailing from the handles.

Light and heavy. That was pretty much how the whole day would play out. As I was being escorted through my various duties—the ceremony itself, quick-hit interviews—I saw Yuki Kawauchi break the tape in the men's race. I loved it: a quirky lifelong underdog who was technically still an amateur, the first Japanese winner in thirty-one years. No one would have bet on the two of us.

Jack and the rest of the BAA organization kept me moving. They were concerned about my physical state, as I was more vulnerable to hypothermia once I slowed down. I tried to take in everything, knowing I shouldn't rush these already fleeting minutes, fighting my primal desire to go inside and get warm.

JOHN BALL WALKED by me in the recovery room at the Fairmont, backpack slung over one shoulder, ready to head for the airport. He never wasted time leaving a race. I was still thawing out, covered with towels on a massage table. We made eye contact. He mouthed, "What the fuck just happened?" with an incredulous expression, then kept walking.

He sent me this text the next day:

> I knew on that bus ride down yesterday that you were going to do something special. When that storm hit during that ride out, I watched everyone else get more and more shaky. You just got calmer and calmer. I thought you'd get a boost from some of the others dropping. I knew you were going to finish and end up well above where you were fitness wise. It wouldn't have produced the same story, but would have been no less

impressive. People always pay tribute to the mental side of sport. Very few actually know what that means. Knowing what you stepped to the line with yesterday and the months leading into it, that was the most impressive thing I've ever watched firsthand in sports. Thanks for letting me sit next to it on the way. Reminded me why I love what I get to do. Woke up in Phoenix much warmer and determined to find more resilience in my own life.

Thanks Des.

AMID THE CHAOS, I ran into Keith Hanson. He asked if he could take a picture. I assumed he wanted a photo of us together, but instead, he stepped back and snapped a shot of me. Just me. It underlined a separation that had never been formalized. This was something I'd pictured with the brothers for so long. It was supposed to be shared.

I told him I was sad that things were the way they were. I meant it.

THE DAY BEFORE the race, Kara had sent me a good-luck text that alluded to my complicated situation with the

Hansons. As a whistleblower in the Salazar-NOP case, she was familiar with the consequences of speaking out.

> I am so impressed by you. You know what
> you stand for and you never waver. There are
> so many people that are inspired by you, you
> have no idea. Have a great race tomorrow. I
> have no doubt that you will. You are such a
> good marathoner. Go get that title!!!

I'd briefly considered telling her about my lowered expectations, then decided against it, and answered in a similar spirit to hers.

> Thanks. Appreciate the message. Excited
> about the American squad, know that you
> got this thing rolling. Hope you're well.

Among the blizzard of texts I received after the race, Kara's reaction stood out.

> Yaaaaas queen! You are so amazing. Soak it
> up!! So happy for you!

AT THE PRESS conference, I was asked what I was thinking during the national anthem.

"I was replaying the whole scenario. At six miles, it was 'No way, not my day.' It's kind of hilarious how it worked out. Even when I got the lead, I thought, *This is gonna go horribly wrong. I'm gonna blow up—chewed up and spit out the back. And then I can drop out.* Then you break the tape, and 'This is not what I expected today.'"

When did I think it was going to be my day?

"When I made the right on Hereford. Honestly, I was running totally afraid. I've been in a sprint on Boylston Street. I tried not to let up on the gas until I hit the tape."

Last words?

"This is hands down the biggest day of my running career, and if it hadn't been difficult, I don't think it would mean as much."

It was all true—at least, as much truth as I was willing to share in that moment.

SHALANE FOUND ME in the lobby. I was conscious of the stares and the cameras rolling around us, but it still felt as if we were in an intimate winner's circle of two. We had come a long way since that crushing morning in Rio, punching through history with back-to-back major championships in our own country.

I gave her a quick recap on what had happened after the bathroom break. She touched the gold medal around my neck, exclaimed over the olive wreath. "It's so pretty, Des," she said, then hugged me. "You're awesome. I'm so proud." She seemed as genuinely excited for me as I had been watching her in New York. I appreciated how gracious Shalane was, given her individual disappointment. Few could understand her career-long quest in Boston the way I did or comprehend what it was like to squeeze through a fast-closing window of opportunity just in time.

I CARVED OUT exactly ten minutes for myself to take a shower. This was the moment I'd anticipated with so much angst—coming back to my room defeated and deflated, on my way out of the sport. The contrast made me smile, alone in the billowing clouds of steam. And then Ryan hollered at me to hurry up. I had to be somewhere. And then somewhere else. For the indefinite future.

Natalie and Brad and my parents were ushered into the room Hancock had set up for lunch. "We're proud of you," they said almost in unison. My dad isn't one to cry, but I saw the emotion in his eyes. I draped my medal around my mom's neck. Natalie, ever the princess, wanted to wear the olive wreath. "Now you have to win again, so we can have two," she said with her usual warm, teasing smile.

MK walked in as we were eating. "Well, it's about time," she said. She was joking on one level, but the joke was layered with truth. We'd been talking about this for years. She had never lost confidence in me.

———

THAT NIGHT, I returned to the scene of my earlier discontent: the postrace party at the Red Lantern restaurant where I had seethed with frustration the year before. I'd been improvising all day, but I had absolutely devoted a minute to premeditate how I would cap the celebration—inspired by Daniel Ricciardo, one of my favorite Formula 1 drivers, who had made "shoeys" a thing. With most of the important people in my life surrounding me, hooting and hollering, I poured a glass of champagne into a lightly worn casual sneaker—left foot, Brooks Fusion in a Birds of Paradise colorway—tipped the toe skyward, and drank.

◆ ◆ ◆

KEITH EMAILED ME a few days later. It was a thoughtful note saying he and Kevin also felt bad about where things stood. He asked if I still wanted them to coach me moving forward— or at the very least, if we could part on a cordial note. I replied that coaching probably wasn't in the cards but maintaining a relationship was important. I suggested that we meet and see where we could land that would be best for everyone.

I recognized that the conversation was way overdue, and that it was mostly my fault. I also knew I'd been remiss not to reach out to Dathan before this. I wanted to make both of those things right.

I HADN'T PACKED my bag thinking I'd be a winner, that I'd have to wake up and do a bunch of morning shows and make a trip to New York for more media. I wore the same pair of jeans for three days straight until Ryan finally went out and bought me some new ones.

A friend had taken a great picture of Ryan in our hotel room, watching the late stages of the race with an enormous grin on his face before he and Josh went out to the finish. To his credit, he hadn't said "I told you so." That didn't mean he was any more prepared than I was for what it would mean.

Nothing truly sank in until we got back to Michigan, picked up the dogs, and packed the car to head north to Charlevoix. The ride was one long, deep breath for both of us. *Holy shit, that just happened.* Life just got cleaved into Before and After.

I MET THE Hansons at their shop in Royal Oak, outside Detroit. The start of the conversation felt oddly normal: rehashing race day, filling them in about the entire experience.

When we pivoted to what I'd said about Dathan, things got predictably uncomfortable. There was nothing to be done about the past and how disappointed I felt when they brought him on. All I could control was my future, and I was direct. I didn't feel I fit into their group anymore, from either a training perspective or a personal perspective. Somewhat to my surprise, they seemed open to other options. Would I stay with the group in name, but with a new coach? We all threw out ideas. I left feeling as if we were belatedly working through things, and called Josh to tell him so.

Josh called me back the same day, confused. He'd heard from Steve DeKoker, a then–Brooks sports marketing manager, who had heard from Kevin, who was insisting that I wear their jersey moving forward because of what they'd done for me. It sent me straight back to that old place of being made to feel indebted, of power imbalance, of the one-way street of gratitude. It also made my decision to leave the ODP easy.

As always, Josh said he would handle the repercussions of whatever I opted to do. With that support in hand, I made the choice to put my own happiness first. Months later, after I had reached out to Walt and he'd agreed to coach me, Brooks CEO Jim Weber took me aside at a party and told me he was glad to hear my new coaching situation was working well. It felt like the kind of individual support I'd always wanted and a different level of trust and partnership from the brand.

I REACHED OUT to Dathan, and he came to our house in Rochester, a class gesture on his part. The specifics of our conversation were private, and I've always kept it that way. I wanted to make it clear that I had no personal ill will toward him, and no interest in pushing him out of the Hansons' group or taking opportunities of any kind away from him. We talked about his experience with Salazar and the Nike Oregon Project. I understood that he was still dealing with an ugly situation that wasn't going to be resolved any time soon. It reaffirmed my initial instinct to move on.

I'D STUFFED MY jacket, headband, and racing flats into a bag moments after I finished the race and handed them off to Josh, not dwelling on their significance. Gloria Ratti requested something for the BAA collection before we left Boston. The jacket and headband went to her, for the same museum I had once viewed as an unattainable sanctum. The shoes went to Brooks headquarters in Seattle.

Weeks later, a heavy, oversized package arrived at our house. Gloria had methodically, lovingly gathered dozens of Boston 2018 news clips, had them reproduced on high-quality stock, and put together giant scrapbooks in two archival boxes. Enclosed was a note typed on BAA letterhead explaining that she used to do this every year until the digital age seemed to make it irrelevant.

But for some reason, I had a bee in my bonnet and asked the staff not to destroy any of the newspapers until after the Boston Marathon, so I was waist high in newspapers following the race.

Imagine my surprise and sheer happiness when you crossed our Finish Line this year in what was the most challenging and difficult race in my many years of association with the Boston Athletic Association.

So, a couple of weeks after the Marathon, I took my scissors in hand and clipped each and every article I could find. There was very little leading up to the elite field until a day or so before the Marathon and then a wonderful "deluge" of articles heralding your momentous win!

So, you are the recipient of a very outdated mode of scrapbook articles for you to store away in your memorabilia closet and with it, fond memories of an event that will never again be repeated.

There are countless reasons I'm glad I won when I did, but very high on the list is getting it done while Gloria was there to see it.

I WOULD NEVER have to wonder whether I'd be invited back to Boston. My face would be on the banners suspended from the lampposts in Back Bay during race week. My name and my result had become permanent entries in a 122-year-old history book. A two-second difference in a sprint down Boylston Street would no longer be the defining moment in my career. I had finally gotten the one that got away.

My 2011 finish in Boston was still my personal best time in the distance, yet it hadn't been enough to win. Seven years later, winning meant the best effort that made sense that day—the same lesson that had been so hard for me to put into practice after my hypothyroidism diagnosis.

In a way, I was circling back to my beginnings as a pro, when all I wanted to do was justify another season of running, more time to make a living while exploring my limits. A year as defending champion carried prestige and financial benefits and ego satisfaction, sure, but what meant the most was having more time. Time to actually get back in shape, time to be patient with myself, time to decide how much longer I might be able to go.

EPILOGUE

WE MAKE THE ninety-degree right turn onto Commonwealth Avenue at the Newton fire station and start going uphill, chasing Ethiopia's Worknesh Degefa, who had soloed away early and built a substantial lead. Edna Kiplagat is there, and Jordan Hasay, and maybe eight or ten others as we approach Mile 18.

I sense it before it actually happens: I can't hang on. I'm off the back, losing ground as the pack strings out. I watch the shoulders bobbing ahead of me get smaller and farther away.

I'm alone. The hardest part of the course is ahead of me. Fatigue, more mental than physical, hits me like a brick.

That's that. I'm done. I just need to get to the finish without falling apart.

Everything about this Boston build has been challenging. Huge opportunity, equally huge sense of responsibility, right up to the prerace press conference where I was presented with the defending champion's bib bearing the number 1. I've put in a lot of time to make the most of it, not only for my own future but also because I was intent on promoting the event and trying to keep the sport front and center. All while I was still acclimating to my body's new reality. I've only recently reached the point where it feels as if I'm able to train like my old self again.

It'll be work to finish in the top ten. I consider my options.

I could back off and just run hard instead of racing it in. Nobody would know the difference.

And then I think of Gabe.

◆ ◆ ◆

I DIDN'T KNOW Gabriele Grunewald well, truthfully. She was a middle-distance specialist who had spent most of the previous ten years in the shadow of a life-threatening illness and had started a foundation devoted to rare cancer research. We'd crossed paths at Brooks events, and, cheesy as it sounds, her attitude embodied the company's #RunHappy slogan—so impressive, given all she'd been through. Her social media posts radiated warmth and determination, and she'd been openly supportive of me. She was very much a glass-half-full person, a worldview I knew I could use more of as I picked my way through the welcome but foreign territory of being defending champion.

My own health had come a long way since the fall of 2017. I'd learned to be meticulous about getting my energy levels back to normal and to be patient when my medication was adjusted. If I felt overly tired, it could be hard to pinpoint the source: Training volume? Business obligations? Thyroid? All of the above? Walt and I tried to manage my workouts to make sure I didn't backslide. I wasn't looking to make huge strides forward in fitness, but I also knew this was about the time frame that John and I had hoped I might be back to where I'd been before my diagnosis, before my symptoms spiraled. Provided I could get there, I knew I would be in the mix as I usually was in April in Boston.

The dueling thoughts of that moment when I stood shivering on the podium became a constant theme in my life: *I need to stand here and soak in what I've done. No, I need to get inside and get warm.* I wanted to celebrate my win and capitalize on it in every way, but I was also driven to claw my way uphill to my former peak fitness. Every time I wanted to turn down a trip, a speaking engagement, a sponsor photo or video shoot, every time I was tempted to ask Josh to clear my calendar, I circled back to the reality that these problems of mine were the greatest problems in the world. It made sense to do as much as I could while I was in demand.

I had picked up a handful of new sponsors that kept me busy in early 2019. Both media requests and asks from John Hancock ratcheted up to new highs as the race approached. I knew it would be near impossible to keep race weekend from becoming overwhelming. One prerace duty I looked forward to was throwing out the ceremonial first pitch at Fenway Park—something I'd done before, including at a Padres game with my parents looking on—but never in Boston as defending champion. Spending a few innings in the stands with Josh and MK afterward would be one of my few respites.

I was feeling worn down and sorry for myself in early April when I scrolled through Twitter and joined an exchange between Gabe and my fellow distance runner Stephanie Bruce.

"Everybody loves a comeback story, but we don't often praise consistency, staying healthy, and stacking multiple training blocks on top of one another," Steph had written, tagging me and a few others.

> GABE: "And sometimes, life happens, and your only choice is a comeback."
> ME: "No doubt. There's certainly reason, and room, to root for all of it. So many inspirations in our sport."
> GABE: "Indeed! And I'm just triggered cuz I miss running and racing so much. I think you all rock."

Her words humbled me. I could almost hear an apologetic tone, as if she needed to explain why she'd been so blunt. Gabe had run her last professional race two years before, in between chemotherapy treatments for adenoid cystic carcinoma, the rare form of cancer that had upended her life. Who was I to feel exhausted? My condition wasn't terminal, and Boston 2018 had bought me time to deal with it. I had a lot of road in front of me to strive for consistency. She didn't have that privilege.

    ME: "Healthy dose of perspective. All my miles for
       you, Gabe."
    GABE: "Not all of them! That's a lot of miles for me,
       Des—too many!"

THE DAY BEFORE the race, sitting onstage at a BAA fan event in Copley Square, I brought up the conversation.

"It was this eye-opening moment," I said. "She can't do this right now. She would love to. We're so fortunate to get to do what we do, and we can make every mile count and matter. I'm gonna give all those miles on Monday to Gabe."

My voice caught on the last part. Saying it out loud made it real. There was no answer for why Gabe was dying and I was whole, yet she was handing me the most powerful "why" of all—for this race, for however long I decided to keep running. She was doing so much more for me than I ever could for her.

◆ ◆ ◆

I snap out of my self-pity. My situation—being dropped, feeling ambivalent about working hard—isn't a problem. It's a luxury.

The last six miles would usually be dedicated to my team, to repay what they had invested in me. Not today. Today they would be for Gabe. I imagine myself finishing, then telling her: *I wanted to quit, but you kept me going.*

I fix my eyes on the back of the runner closest to me and pick up my pace, feeling the familiar burn of the Newton hills. I pass her. I take aim at the next figure in the distance.

◆ ◆ ◆

October 26, 2020

Day twenty-six of the Destober Calendar Club. The day everyone expects me to run a full marathon.

I'm 325 miles into this challenge I put out into the world, committing myself to run the number of miles equivalent to each date: 2 miles on October 2, 10 miles on October 10, and so on. The response has been strong on social media;

seven months into the pandemic, people are clearly glad to have a daily goal, whether they're counting miles or kilometers or minutes of activity.

It's been a great collaborative project with Brooks that took the question marks out of my day. All I had to do was get up and run what was on the schedule. As I ticked off the early, easy workouts, I realized how much I had missed fresh motivation and structure.

But at home in Charlevoix this afternoon, I'm paying the price. I'm moving like a rusty robot. Everything aches, creaks, and feels a little stuck, especially, but not limited to, my hips, knees, and ankles.

I've been doing the mileage in one shot each day thus far, but planned to split things into two-a-days at some point. Now I'm seeing a terrible flaw in that plan.

Ryan and I ran sixteen miles in the morning, and it went by in a blink, but every cell in my body rebels at the idea of pushing out the door for another ten. My teenage self who balked at my dad's insistence that we hit the Silver Strand before sundown is fully activated. All I want is to curl up on the couch with my golden retriever and a book.

Remind me again why I'm doing this?

◆ ◆ ◆

IN MY MIND, I'm still only as good as my last race. Winning Boston hasn't changed that.

The race that turned out to be my last of 2020 really stung.

I lined up at the Olympic trials on February 29 after a difficult buildup, feeling as if I could finish anywhere from first to fifteenth. The field was deep and bunched closely in ability—a recipe for unpredictable outcomes. I ran as well as I could have expected on the hilly course in Atlanta and wound up missing the team by eleven seconds: fourth place, first loser. As the missed opportunity started to sink in, I was a little surprised at how much it hurt. At least I had Boston to aim for again.

Just two weeks later, Covid-19 was rampaging through the country, and sports, along with everything else, shut down. I checked in with John Ball. "I think everything's going to be canceled for a year minimum, maybe a year and a half," he said. As usual, he was right. Boston was initially rescheduled for September, then scrubbed, as were the rest of the majors. The International Olympic Committee dithered but finally postponed Tokyo 2020 for a year.

Any issues in my running life obviously paled in comparison to what was afflicting the world, but I needed to think strategically. Running was my primary source of income, and I was in my peak earning years. I wasn't exactly unemployed, but the most important part of my job had suddenly vanished. If everything had gone as planned, I would have run three marathons—trials, Boston, Tokyo—in five months. I tried to look at the upside. I could take a long break and avoid digging myself into a hole again the way I did in 2017.

I was also the first Olympic alternate. I didn't wish misfortune on any of the three qualifiers, and I had gone on record as saying that I didn't think the trials should be rerun. Yet being realistic, the delay meant more variables in what could happen. I needed to be ready, and I needed something to kick-start me down the road. As I approached negotiation time at the end of a contract year, I wanted to find other ways to be meaningful and valuable to Brooks in the absence of competition.

While Ryan and I were hunkered down in Charlevoix that summer, our friend Travis McKenzie, a triathlete and ultramarathoner, participated in a Calendar Club to raise money for the Dempsey Center cancer care and support facility in Maine. Ryan and I found ourselves super-interested and invested in his progress. How would we handle that kind of mileage? At what point would we break up the distance into two or even three runs a day?

It was clear that people missed the communal aspect of running and racing. In my conversations with Brooks, the goal was to engage runners in an event that could take the place of fall marathons. We wanted to inspire and challenge—*What's motivating you right now?*—but also build a shared experience, as if we were heading out for a group run every day. Brooks would take charge of branding the event and all of the social media content, and I'd handle the running.

Based on a back-of-the-napkin calculation, my lifetime odometer had ticked well above 80,000 by this time. Destober would tack on 496 miles. The number didn't seem that daunting until I was facing down those last few days and fully grasped the implications of a 196-mile week, following a 147-miler, which was around 20 more than I'd ever done. It was a peak I'd never seen, and that unknown was the whole point, but I couldn't help wondering how thin the air would feel.

◆ ◆ ◆

THERE'S ONLY SO much time to procrastinate, even for a skilled procrastinator like me. Eventually Ryan and I decide it's time to lace up and get it over with. I hate the mentality.

We head for Clipperview, a curving, paved road that rises gradually but steadily for the first two miles and is tough on my already achy joints. As we grind up this route I love to hate, I tell myself that pace doesn't matter. The goal is to cover the distance and enjoy—in bulk—the process of running. Savoring the hardest moments is what I've signed up for over and over again. The aches ease away, and I find myself appreciating the chance to mindlessly put one foot in front of the other.

It's hunting season for turkey and deer—arguably Ryan's

favorite time of year. The fall foliage is brilliant, and we catch glimpses of Lake Michigan as we crest hills on dirt roads we've never run before. Ryan launches into his usual stream-of-consciousness conversation that always keeps me thinking and entertained. One minute it'll be a comment on the mechanics of a piece of farm equipment we just saw, and the next minute he'll move on to work or politics or our dogs. Anything is fair game. We've run mileage equivalent to multiple times around the planet, and yet we've never run out of things to discuss.

The pandemic has put travel and racing and so much of what I took for granted on hold, but I still have this. I settle into a racing frame of mind: run the mile I'm in, stay present. I also know it's the only way I'll get to the first of November.

We're lucky. We're healthy.

This is why.

◆ ◆ ◆

April 13, 2021

I'VE RUN 26.2 miles in 2:31:12, I have 5 more miles to go, and I'm running in the opposite direction of where I need to end up.

That's been the plan all along on this flat course along a lake in western Oregon—a closed course with two longer loops that add up to marathon distance, and then a shorter out-and-back to bring me to 31.06 miles, or the more magical round number of 50 kilometers. It's been designed for me to try to notch the fastest time in the world.

It also means that on this segment, as I race farther than I've ever raced before, I'm actually heading away from the finish line. A total mind-fuck.

And the brain? Rattling off questions, spinning at a rate that's surely burning precious glycogen.

Did I take in enough nutrition? Were the quicker middle miles too quick? Will they catch up to me now?

My goal has been to run 5:45s all day. I got a little ambitious and clicked off a few 5:40s between Miles 13 and 19, then split 5:34 at Mile 21. These few seconds aren't trivial—they're potential mistakes that can snowball into an avalanche.

I glance at my watch. My pace has slipped from mid 5:40s to the high 5:50s.

I need to get myself to the turnaround point. That's my next finish line. I can't think about anything else.

My legs are feeling heavy and shaky underneath me, and the popping sensation of my feet leaving the ground that was there in the early miles has vanished. I feel like I'm slogging through ankle-deep puddles now.

As I'm telling myself to keep it together, I feel myself leaking more time, slowly at first, then all at once, like a boat taking on water. I'm hurting in a way that I haven't felt in forever, since the marathon was new and unpredictable for me. I'm uncertain how this will unfold. And I love it.

◆ ◆ ◆

THE YEAR HAD begun with another slew of canceled races, another Boston off the table. Time for me and Josh to think creatively again. When I signed my new contract with Brooks, there was an understanding that I would eventually transition from traditional road racing to trail and ultradistance events: an ideal way to enhance my career, keep my sponsor visible, and satisfy my continuing curiosity about my outer limits. This was a chance to scout out that next chapter.

The 50k was a logical target—a few miles longer than the marathon but not an outlandish number. The fastest women's time to date was 3:07:20, set by Alyson Dixon of Great Britain in the fall of 2019. It was considered a "world best" by the International Association of Ultrarunners. Our goal was to have it recognized as a formal world record by World Athletics, the governing body for track and field.

Josh and I talked through logistics for the attempt. April made sense, since it was the time I would traditionally race in the spring. In order for my time to be considered an official world record, we needed to meet a few requirements. We brought in USADA to conduct drug testing, hired a respected course designer and certifier, and settled on the venue: the Row River Road bike path along Dorena Lake, where the foothills of the Cascade Mountains give way to more level land thirty miles south of Eugene. Under international rules, five athletes—counting me, at least two women—had to finish at the 50k distance on the same course that day. Ryan would be one. Ultrarunner Sally McRae and local runners Miriam Udosenata and Jenn Lewis agreed to participate, as did my friend Nick Thompson, CEO of *The Atlantic* magazine, who was chasing the forty-five-and-over age group record. To complete the group, we reached out to Charlie Lawrence, who I knew from the Rochester area. He was training for the 50k nationals at the time, and I'd had enough beverages with him to know that he'd be good company.

WHEN WE ANNOUNCED the attempt, much of the running public reacted as if it were low-hanging fruit. Dixon's time wasn't outrageously fast, and my consistency over the years led people to think that all I'd have to do was recalibrate my pace. I knew there was a lot more to it, and no guarantee that things would connect in training or come together on race day.

I worked with Walt to map out a plan. I would spend the early part of the year in Charlevoix, a month in Arizona, and apply the finishing touches in Rochester—very similar to a Boston build. My peak mileage relative to marathon training would go down, which seemed counterintuitive, but my 110 to 115 miles a week would be more targeted, with a higher percentage of miles at race-pace effort. I'd make sure to redial in the basics, locking into a rhythm and training my gut again by consuming fluids as I would during a race—skills I hadn't had to be intentional about training in years.

I extended my long run every few weeks, from my previous high of 20 miles to 22, then 24, and, finally, about a month out, a 26-miler with 3 × 5 miles at 50k race pace within the run. I knew that one would be a crucial gauge of my fitness.

On my second day in Arizona, we drove out to our secret training spot, in a popular mountain biking area crisscrossed with desert trails. My route would be out and back on a 5-mile stretch of rolling road with a wide shoulder and low traffic.

My training log told the story.

48 DEGREES, SUNNY, 4 MPH ESE WIND

PRESCRIBED WORKOUT:
6-mile warm-up
3 × 5 miles at race pace
2 miles easy recovery between sets
1 mile cooldown

ACTUAL WORKOUT:

6-mile warm-up

set 1: 5:42, 5:37, 5:32, 5:35, 5:46

set 2: 5:26, 5:47, 5:34, 5:32, 5:29

set 3: 5:33, 5:31, 5:26, 5:36, 5:48

1.2 mile cooldown to hit the marathon distance

TOTAL ELEVATION: 1,207 FEET

2:36:17 FOR 26.2 MILES

I'M READY.

My confidence and mood surged as I showered off the dust. Josh and I celebrated by heading to a Padres spring training game. I kick-started recovery with a Pacífico tallboy and a ballpark hot dog—icing on a rare, perfect training day.

I began to think the record was a slam dunk and breaking the three-hour barrier was a real possibility. I'd have to average roughly 5:45 per mile to knock it down, and I had the work to back up my belief—so much so that I decided to put that idea out into the universe. All the pieces were falling into place.

One aspect of race day that would be very different was the absence of spectators. We had to make the event Covid safe, but I didn't want to feel totally isolated, so I decided to reunite my race-weekend crew. Josh, Ryan, and I rented a house in Eugene and started filling it with some of our favorite people. Covid-related cabin fever was rampant by this time, and the prospect of a fun few days with group dinners and a common goal was irresistible. Josh brought his wife, Carrie, and associate Larry Rosenblatt. MK said, "Hell, yes," as soon as I brought it up, and we included Billy Yang, an independent filmmaker who would be capturing content.

IF A RECORD falls in the woods, and nobody is there to see it, does it make noise? Our goal was to make that answer a yes.

◆ ◆ ◆

I HIT THE last turnaround with two and a half miles to go. As I come around the orange cone and finally point myself toward the finish line, I realize brain fog has descended. It reminds me of that bottom-of-the-well feeling I had before my thyroid diagnosis—a heaviness, mind not quite connected to body. After many miles of running even with Charlie Lawrence, I'm lagging a little behind him. He slows just enough to come shoulder to shoulder.

"Let's go, Des! Finish this!" I hear him say.

I know how to manage this. In fact, I know how to do it better than anyone.

Show up, one step at a time.

I do some murky math. I've got the world record locked up, but I'm going to be incredibly close to the three-hour mark. I could settle and still crush the record. Who would know or care if I gave up for the last few minutes?

No. I know there's more there.

I'm willing to hurt a little bit longer to find out just how much, because it won't be nearly as painful as missing sub–three hours by a second or two. This straightaway is my new Boylston Street, forcing me to throttle up when I'm on fumes and sprint for what I want. The process has taught me that I can always give myself one more thing to chase down.

I pull my body out of its slumping stride and push forward, rising up on my toes, to launch into what would be considered a kick for an ultramarathoner.

I can see the clock in the distance—2:59:40 . . . 41 . . . 42 . . .

My mind clears. I've made my choice.

2:59:50 . . .

"Awesome," I tell Charlie. "Let me take it."

ACKNOWLEDGMENTS

This book is the product of a group of bright, talented, hardworking people coming together to turn my harebrained ideas into something respectable. I'm proud of the finished product, but I'm far prouder to have the privilege of working with such amazing individuals. Relationships are everything. Thank you to everyone who had a hand in making this project come to life. It's better because of you.

Special thanks to:

My editor Jill Schwartzman, and the entire team at Dutton. Jill, I appreciate the enthusiasm and passion you brought to this project every single time we connected. Thank you for pushing me a little beyond my comfort zone and dragging out the right words and stories that made this book authentic.

My literary agent Anna Petkovich, and the Park & Fine agency, for fielding my first call so long ago and being willing to take me on as a client. Thank you for believing in my story and always going to bat for my ideas. Not sure "agent" accurately captures the jobs you take on and the amount of effort you put in—I truly appreciate it.

To the Brooks Running team for the seventeen years of support. No partnership is perfect, but ours feels pretty dang close—and we're working on some of our best chapters yet. To Jim Weber, thank you for sharing your own publishing experience and offering hard-earned knowledge and advice about the process.

Bonnie Ford, you're the best at your craft and it was an absolute pleasure to work with you and see the process behind your brilliance. It's easy to pin you as a natural, but watching you turn my messy brain dumps into something interesting and entertaining was nothing short of miraculous. Thank you for your hard work, patience, kindness, and honesty. There is no one else I could have done this project with, and it's an honor to call you a friend. Also, a big thanks to Bob, and your entire family, for letting me steal so much of your time.

Barbara Huebner, you are the unsung hero of this project. Thanks for reading so many drafts, helping me grapple with a number of sticky sections, saving me from many embarrassing mistakes, and teaching me how to use adverbs properly—properly use adverbs? Ah, hell. Most important, thanks for always being someone I can turn to, no matter the topic. I'm beyond lucky to have you in my corner.

Kate Gustafson, I appreciate you reading draft after draft with fresh eyes and valuable feedback. There's nothing quite like a run around Manhattan catching up with you and kicking around ideas, many of which made it into this book.

Josh, there are not enough words. We've shared so many hours and beers talking about my running career and what it would be like when I won the Boston Marathon. It didn't wind up looking anything like we'd dreamed of, but that made it a bit more special. I appreciate all your support as an agent, but more important, as a friend. Thanks for recognizing that this version, the full version, of my Boston win needed to be told, and helping me align another perfect team to get the job done. I know there will be many more game-changing projects in our future.

Mom and Dad, thanks for loving me in your own way—I haven't always understood it, but I've never doubted that it comes from the heart. I appreciate everything you've done for me and feel so fortunate to have been given every opportunity to be a success. I hope you take pride in what I've accomplished. And to my in-laws, Cathy and Len, it has meant so much to have you jump in and become such loyal fans of my career. Cathy, we've come a long way from the time you asked me, "Don't you get bored being unemployed?" Seriously, thank you for supporting my unconventional career path.

Natalie, thanks for being the world's best teammate. Thanks for going first, paving the way, and never settling.

You personify "Keep showing up." I'm grateful for your example. I look forward to many more adventures ahead. And Brad, there's nobody else I'd want her to force onto my fan bandwagon.

Ryan, none of this happens without you. Thank you for all your love and support. I'm not sure where I'd be without it and I'd rather not find out. Love you.

ABOUT THE AUTHOR

Des Linden grew up in San Diego, graduated from Arizona State University, and has been a professional runner since 2006. She is a two-time Olympian, won the Boston Marathon in 2018, and currently holds the women's 50k world record. A bourbon and coffee aficionado, she lives with her husband, Ryan, in Michigan.